THE CHRISTMAS DILEMMA

GATES POINT

LYNN STORY

The Christmas Dilemma

Lynn Story

Copyright © 2024 Lynn Story

All rights reserved. No part of this book may be reproduced, stored in a retrieval system, or transmitted in any form or by any means—electronic, mechanical, photocopying, recording, or otherwise—without the prior written permission of the publisher, except for brief quotations used in reviews or other critical works.

This is a work of fiction. Names, characters, places, and incidents either are products of the author's imagination or are used fictitiously. Any resemblance to actual events, locales, or persons, living or dead, is entirely coincidental.

Published by Stitches and Stories

For more information, visit www.stitchesandstories.com

Cover Design by Lynn Story

For Larry, Always.

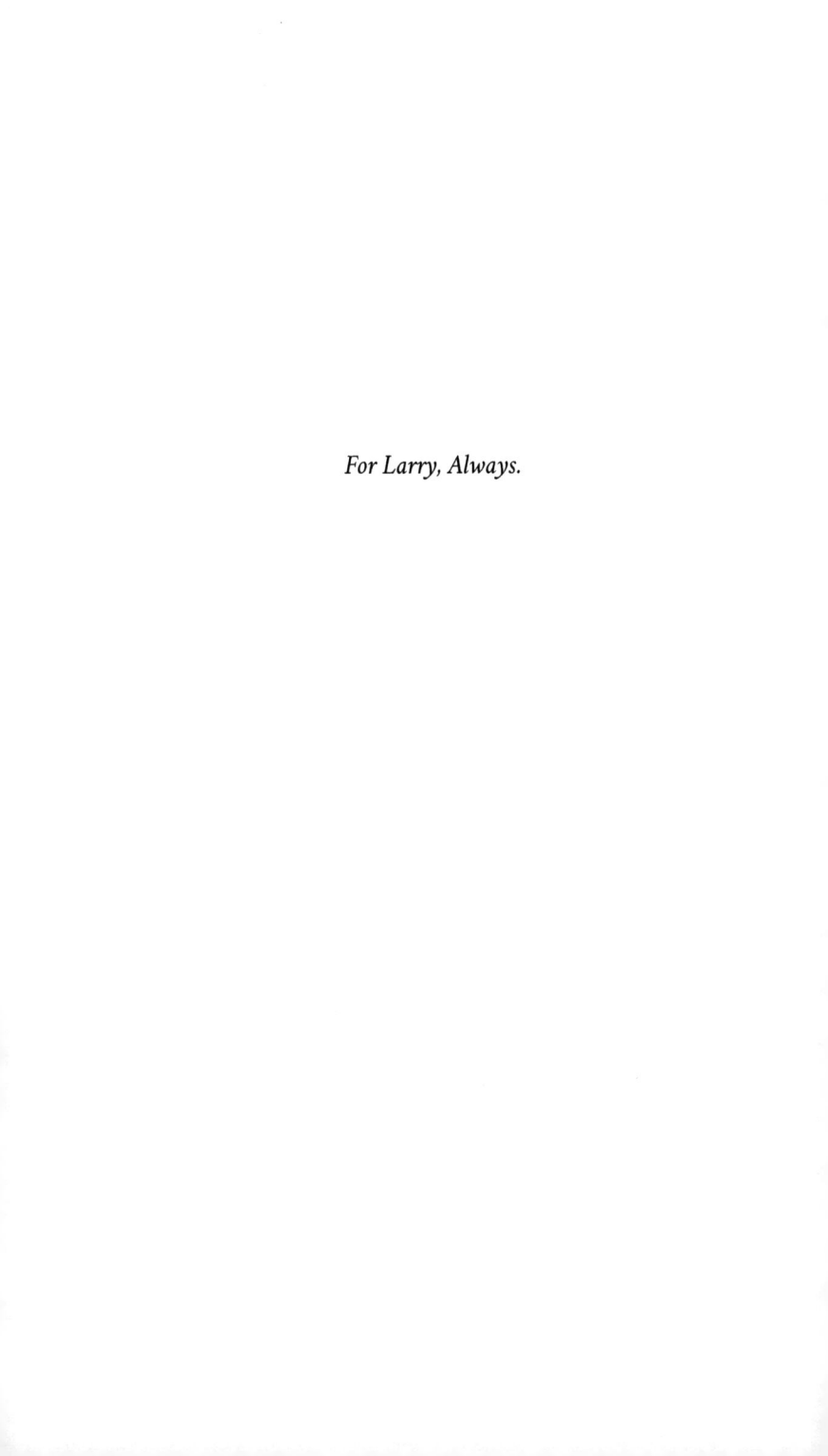

CHAPTER 1

*H*arper

December 1st

The TV screen glowed in the corner of my bedroom. The familiar bumper music of the weather report drew me from the bathroom with my toothbrush still in my mouth. My final decision about what to wear today depended on what the perky brunette said next.

"A polar vortex drops low and brings freezing temperatures and the possibility of snow to Gates Point. The weather will have everyone staying indoors. Of course, the question on everyone's mind, will we see snow and how will it impact the holiday festival this weekend? Back to you Jim and Kate."

I sighed, stepping back into the bathroom. Snow was rare in Gates Point. Being so close to the Atlantic Ocean often kept the temperatures above freezing, which made it feel magical when we got snow—but as the event coordinator for the holiday festival, it also meant bracing for long hours outside. I needed to dress for the cold.

The idea of winter weather added nothing to my mood this morning. I was already dreading a meeting to discuss the festival budget. I despise this part of my job. The city is inconsistent with how much financial support they provide, and it makes it harder to plan for the event. I've secured a couple of large sponsors, but we still need more. Checking the time, I rush to get dressed. I want to get to the office early.

Opting for warm boots with black wool slacks and a soft pink sweater, I grab my laptop. Just as I was about to walk out the door, my phone chirped with a text message from my best friend, Christina. "Lunch today?"

"Yes, I have a feeling I am going to need it." I typed back, juggling my laptop, coffee, keys, and phone.

Her emoji reply made me smile. Finally, I stepped out onto the sidewalk, only to be greeted by heavy slate gray clouds rolling in from the northwest. The creaking of the bare branches of the street trees sounded like they were scratching the sky as they strained against the icy wind.

Fighting against the wind as I hurried up the sidewalk, the two blocks from my apartment in the central district to city hall only took ten minutes. I was the first person to arrive this morning, so I went to the kitchenette to start the coffee and then set up the conference room for the meeting.

Marla, my administrative assistant, called out as she came through the door. "Morning Harper, I'll set up the conference room."

"I already did, and I started the coffee," I answered. She poked her head in, grinning. "Love that sweater, Harper. Perhaps it will help charm a few extra pennies out of Daniel Stewart for the celebration."

I couldn't help but laugh. Marla had a warm and infectious smile.

"You're ridiculous!" I shot back, rolling my eyes. Bringing up the files I would need for the meeting before gathering my laptop and refilling my coffee. I had five minutes to spare as I headed to the conference room. Staff members began arriving. Daniel Stewart, Budget Director, arrived last, looking as meticulous as ever in a dark suit, with a laptop, and coffee in hand. His efficiency was unmatched, and his strict budgeting made him my holiday nemesis.

Once everyone was seated, I took a deep breath and began the meeting. "Morning, everyone. Thanks for braving the cold. Let's dive in."

I launched into my presentation, highlighting our major sponsor, Port City Industries. "Kay Dandridge is our most loyal sponsor, this year she has pledged an additional $20,000," I paused and glanced around the table, "with increased cost in services this still leaves us ten thousand dollars short." I clicked through to the next slide, comparing this year's and last year's budgets.

Daniel leaned in, frowning at the numbers. I braced myself.

"Harper, we're already stretched thin. We can't afford to add another $10,000 to the festival budget at this late date. We have to prioritize—books for the library, equipment for emergency services, or holiday lights. What do you think our citizens value more?"

"Why not all the above?" I countered, keeping my voice level despite the rising frustration. "We're running a balanced budget, aren't we? And these celebrations are for the citizens, too."

Daniel glanced at his screen. "Do you have any room where you could cut back? Advertising costs, or could you get an additional sponsor?" He said, reviewing the breakdown of the event expenses.

Challenging Daniel, I asked, "I'm not sure what we could cut. Most of the additional cost is for staff overtime. It isn't like we are going overboard. We have followed all the purchasing procedures, put out bids for goods and services to ensure we get the best price. Some items are on a multiyear contract, so the prices are locked in. But some services that we have to purchase annually have increased their prices. I don't know what else we can do?"

A murmur of disapproval swept through the room. I took a deep breath and refocused. "Alright, team, any creative ideas to close this gap?"

Suggestions started flying—approaching fraternal organizations, local TV stations...., everyone was talking at once.

I put my hands up to calm the conversation. "let's each follow up with our contacts," I said, wrapping up. "Send me your ideas, and we'll take it from there."

As we packed up, I made it a point to avoid Daniel. He always managed to push my buttons, and I needed to take a deep breath before dealing with him again. Once I was back in my office. I checked on other holiday related tasks, ensuring staff were still on track to get the last lights up around the central district. Satisfied I had done everything I could do at the moment from my desk, I grabbed my coat and headed out into the cold to check the progress of the temporary ice-skating rink, the installation of the tree and the lights.

Two hours later, I plopped down in a chair at Baby Cakes Bakery and Coffee Shop on the other side of the central district square. The sweet aroma of sugar greeted me, wrapping me in safety and comfort like a warm blanket. I believed it was impossible to be unhappy in my mom's bakery. But today might prove to be the exception.

Christina was waiting for me. "Boy, you look grumpy."

"Hello to you too." I snapped.

"Hi," she eyed me warily. "How's your day?"

"Peachy."

"Hi, baby cakes," my mom said, kissing the top of my head.

"Hi mom."

"Rough morning, dear?"

I sighed. "The usual, fighting for more money." I peeled off my coat and hat. "It is really getting cold out there."

"I'll bring you some coffee to warm you up."

"Sugar, I need sugar!" I called after her.

Christina gave me a sympathetic look. "That bad?"

"That guy Daniel irks me. How can any man that good looking be that annoying?"

Christina rolled her eyes in solidarity. "Aren't all the good-looking ones? I mean, it is like a cruel joke from the universe. Here's a gorgeous man, but he is also overly full of himself!" She sighed, "So, he still won't give you the money?"

"No, he said he claims he adjusted the budget for inflation, but I need to come up with ten thousand dollars on my own! How am I supposed to do that? It isn't like I'm spending it on frivolous items. I have to cover the cost of staff over time for installation, security, fire, and EMS at the actual event. What am I supposed to do?"

Mom reappeared with coffee and one of her baby cakes, aka a cupcake, for both Christina and me.

"Oh mom, you're a lifesaver!"

She laughed, "I know," then moved on to help another customer.

Taking a bite of her cupcake, Christina moaned. "That is so good!"

"You know what? I don't feel the least bit guilty about

having a cupcake for lunch." I savored the chocolate frosting. "The frosting is so good I don't need the cake part."

Christina's phone buzzed. "Oh, our takeout order is ready." She stood up.

"Need any help?"

She shook her head. "No, I'll be right back." She dashed next door to pick up Chinese food for the two of us and mom.

I didn't want to eat takeout in the cafe's dining room, so I took our coffee to mom's office. Having lunch with mom and Christina is something I tried to do whenever I got a real lunch break, which was almost impossible this time of year. But I made time today. I needed to warm up and I need girl time.

As I inhaled the aroma of the takeout, my stomach rumbled. Working as a team, mom and I cleared her desk and set out place settings while Christina unpacked the food.

"How's your day, mom?"

"Oh, nothing special. The flour delivery guy is raising his rates. The health inspector will be here all day tomorrow. I'm down one employee because Kimberly is out with a cold or something."

I felt guilty for having focused on my own problems. "Anything I can do to help?" I offered.

"Oh no thanks sweetie, you have enough on your plate right now. Besides being short on money, how is the holiday planning going?"

"Well, the new program for the Christmas tree should be ready in the next day or so. I just walked past there, and they were testing the program, so that seems on track."

We had invested in a large programmable tree that allowed us to change the music and light patterns every fifteen minutes.

"The skating rink is being installed as we speak. The

lights at the botanical garden were completed this morning. Santa will arrive at the end of the parade, then make appearances in the central district, downtown, and at all the libraries and community centers. I still need to send out e-tickets to staff and sponsor personnel."

My mom fussed. "I worry you're taking on too much, Harper."

"You know how much I love Christmas. Sure, it's a lot of work, and I complain about the budget, but I can't imagine doing anything else. Some of my happiest childhood memories are centered on Christmas."

"I hate seeing you so stressed over it, though."

"I just want to do a good job, Mom."

"You've already done that."

"But I want Gates Point to have the best Christmas light show in Virginia!"

"Why? Can't it just be fun, does it have to be all of that?" Mom argued.

"Wouldn't you like to see this place turned into a holiday wonderland?" I countered, surprised by my mother's stance, knowing she loved Christmas more than I did.

"Not if it means more traffic."

I looked at Christina for help, but all I got was a sympathetic smile and a shrug.

"So, you agree with her?" I asked.

"She makes a good point, but I'm sure traffic control is something you could build into the plan."

"Don't you all remember what it was like when," I almost said when, dad was alive. I didn't want to upset my mother, so instead, I focused on Christina. "When we were kids?" Christina and I had been friends since elementary schools. She was more of a sister than a friend.

"Aw!" My mother came over and hugged me. "I'm not trying to rain on your parade."

"Don't say things like that, mother! Take it back, quickly!"

"What?"

"Don't say rain and parade in the same sentence." I admonished.

Staring up at the ceiling, she said. "I wish for nothing but perfect parade weather for you." She said, hugging me again.

We avoided the topic of the festival for the rest of lunch. When we were done, and everything was cleared away, I turned to give my mom a hug.

"Thank you, I have to go back to work, talk later?"

"Yes, now go. Do good things."

Christina stood, and my mom hugged her, too. "Christina why don't you come for dinner sometime and you can tell me what is going on at the library? Don't wait for my daughter to bring you. Come over any time."

"Thank you, Ms. Wade."

"Girl, you've known me long enough to call me Judy."

Christina nodded, and we both left. Once on the sidewalk, we hugged and went our separate ways. I swear the temperature had dropped ten degrees the hour we were in the bakery. I probably should have ordered soup for dinner and taken it home.

By the time I got back, the energy in the office was buzzing.

"What's going on?" I asked the receptionist.

"Storm is coming. They are sending us to home early."

I pulled my cell phone from my coat pocket. I had missed the email from the City Manager's office.

"Honestly?" I raced to my office to retrieve my laptop and any other essentials I would need to work from home in case we actually got snow.

Back out on the sidewalk again, the clouds had thickened, and a single snowflake landed on my coat sleeve. Snow in December was practically unheard of in Gates Point, but I guess the meteorologist had been right this morning. The thought of it filled me with a schoolgirl's excitement—visions of a cozy day off, binge-watching movies and indulging in guilt-free snacks. But by the time I reached my apartment, reality crept in. Snow could throw the parade and all our holiday festivities into chaos, and I felt the worry settle in the pit of my stomach.

CHAPTER 2

aniel

As I walked to the Holiday Festival budget meeting, the soft sound of Christmas music emanated from staff cubicles. I let out an unintended groan. I enjoy Christmas as much as anyone, but today the music felt mocking, reminding me of the tight budget for the upcoming events. Taking a few calming breaths, I braced myself to face Harper Wade. Trying to see things from her perspective—organizing a multi-day event for the entire city couldn't be easy. But Harper always expected miracles, and when it came to the numbers, reality fell short. Harper and her team didn't differ from any other department asking for more funds, but she had a way of rankling me like no one else. If she asked for more money, I'd have to tell her no.

When I arrived, Harper was already absorbed in her laptop. The frown on her face was at odds with the softness of her pink sweater. I was surprised she hadn't chosen something more festive to wear. Perhaps I was being too judgmental. After all, she was just trying to organize the holiday festival, the same way I was trying to balance the city's budget.

Harper didn't put up much of a fight over the money, which caught me off guard. She suggested everyone get creative for other funding sources. Still, her attitude turned noticeably frosty toward me by the end of the meeting.

I slipped out of the conference room as soon as I could, avoiding any further confrontation with her.

"That didn't take long," Shelly said when I returned to the office.

"Doesn't take long to tell people no," I groused.

She made a noise as I was closing my door. That sounded like, "tsk tsk."

Sinking down into my office chair, I sighed. I'd write Harper a check myself if I could.

An email from the city manager popped up, alerting department heads because of the immediate threat of inclement weather, all city offices would close early.

"Terrific."

There was a mountain of work to do and now I was going to have to do it myself if I was going to meet deadlines. I sent out an email to the supervisors in my office, letting them know about the closing before the city-wide email came out and chaos ensued.

Living within two miles of the office, I normally walked to work, which made it easy to get home on days like today when everyone left the central district at once clogging the streets traffic.

Shelly poked her head in. "Daniel, aren't you leaving? It is going to snow soon."

"I'll leave in a little while. I walked to work, so I'll be fine. But you go before the roads are bad."

Shelly studied me for a moment. "Are you okay?"

"Just a lot to do and closing early doesn't help."

"I can stay if you want." She offered.

That was Shelly, always willing to go the extra mile.

Returning her smile, "No, you go. Be safe."

"Okay, I'll have my laptop. If you need anything, send me a text or something."

"Thanks. I appreciate it. I'll do that."

She gave me a warm smile and left. The department was silent—no music, no hum of desk fans, and no undercurrent of chatter. The solitude was almost unnerving. Glancing out the window; the sky was a dark gray, and a single snowflake landed on the glass. I stared at it, waiting for it to melt. Below, people hurried along the sidewalk, a few carrying umbrellas. Cars choked the streets in slow-moving traffic as other offices in the central district closed along with city hall. I wondered if Harper was one of the people in the crowd below.

As I looked down the street towards the central park, I noticed work had stopped on the ice rink—on the verge of completion, yet empty. I smiled at the irony, the perfect weather for skating, and it just sat there. My mind drifted to the Christmas gifts I'd ordered for my nieces and nephews. Pulling out my phone, I checked the tracking. A quick sigh of relief: they'd arrive in time. I turned back to the computer and all the unread emails. Gloomy skies blurred the time, so when the security guard passed by on his rounds, I jumped.

"Sorry, Mr. Stewart, I didn't mean to startle you."

"Oh, that's okay. I was concentrating and didn't hear you come in."

"What are you doing here so late? Everyone is gone. Aren't you worried about getting home in this weather?"

"No, I don't live too far away. I can walk home. I'll be fine."

The guard seemed to want to say more, but didn't. "Well, have a good night."

"You, too." I checked the time. It was nearly six o'clock. I gazed out the window, but it was so dark, I only saw my reflection. It was time to call it a day. Gathering up my laptop and my overcoat, I headed for the elevator.

A second security guard sat at the desk in the lobby and called out as I went by.

"Good night, stay safe, Mr. Stewart."

I waved good night as I waited for the click of the door lock before pushing it open. Ice pellets stung my face. Turning up the collar of my overcoat, I put my head down and made my way up the sidewalk. It was three blocks up and one block over to the Parkside neighborhood, a collection of old, mostly Victorian homes on River Road. My house remained three blocks away. A few restaurants were still open, and I could see through the windows they were full. The walk home was more treacherous than I had expected and the thought of dinner before going home suddenly seemed like an excellent idea. I was just a few doors away from my favorite restaurant, Marios.

"Ah, evening, Daniel, are you just leaving work?" Anna Maria greeted me as I stepped inside, allowing the warmth to envelop me.

"Yes, no rush to go home when you don't have to drive." I smiled. Anna Maria was Mario's sister. She appeared to be about ten years older than me, with a beautiful Italian accent.

"You're not the only one. The weather is good for business." She said, showing me to a small table off to the side. "Is this okay?"

"Yes, this is perfect." It was a small round table. I put my laptop bag in the chair on the other side and sat down as she disappeared.

Anna Maria returned with her usual warm smile. "Long

day at work?" Her accent wrapped around the words like a comforting blanket.

"Long enough," I replied, trying to match her cheerfulness but falling short. "Calzone tonight, I think." I ate dinner here twice a week, so I had the menu memorized.

She raised an eyebrow; her smile growing mischievous. "Calzone, eh? Comfort food for a troubled mind?"

I forced a smile, "No troubles."

"Ah, Daniel, you are a terrible liar." She leaned in a bit, lowering her voice conspiratorially. "I've seen that look before. My brother Mario wears it when something—or someone—is weighing on him. You work too hard, *caro*. It's Christmas, a time to relax, *sì*?"

I shrugged, unsure how to respond. "Work doesn't stop for the holidays." I didn't argue the point that Christmas was still several weeks away.

"No, but the heart ought to."

Before I could respond, she winked and added, "Your calzone will be out soon. And maybe something sweet to lift your spirits?"

She walked away, her words lingering in the air. As I sat, surrounded by the warmth of the restaurant and the distant murmur of conversations, my thoughts drifted to Harper. I thought of her frustration in the meeting, and to the way her pink sweater seemed so at odds with her serious expression. Maybe she has a softer side?

Anna Maria returned with the calzone, placing it in front of me with a flourish. "Here you go, comfort on a plate. And Daniel," she added, her voice softening, "whatever it is, don't let it weigh you down. Christmas is about finding joy, even in the smallest things."

Glancing around the room. Suits of various kinds filled the tables. Office workers from the surrounding buildings laughing and enjoying an early end to the day and no doubt a day off tomorrow. Anna Maria was right, of course. So, I pushed work to the back of my brain and focus on enjoying my dinner.

My thoughts drifted back to Harper. There was something about her that nagged at me, something I couldn't quite figure out. What was her story? Did she enjoy her job, or was it just another duty she handled with the same determined professionalism she always displayed? I realized, with a pang of guilt, that I'd never considered what else she might deal with throughout the year. The holiday event was just one of many, but it was the only one that brought us into each other's orbit. Why did she get under my skin the way she did?

A three-piece band began setting up in the corner, and I smiled. Mario was making the most of the weather to earn a little extra money, and I admired him for it.

After finishing my meal, I sat back, listening to the music for a while. Anna Maria brought me coffee and cannoli. She was right—the night demanded she stay and savor the atmosphere.

When I finally stepped out of Mario's, the ice had relented, leaving the snow fall in earnest, blanketing the city in a quiet white. Thoughts of Harper consumed me on the walk home. There was something more to her story—I could feel it, but I didn't know what. I decided from now on, I'd stop avoiding her. I needed to understand what made Harper Wade tick and why she annoyed me so much. It was time to see her outside of the budget meetings—time to discover if the woman behind the holiday lights was equally bright and warm. Or was she cold and harsh like the ice pellets that had mixed with the snow earlier?

Once home, sitting in front of a warm fire, I poured myself a glass of wine, feeling a strange mix of anticipation and unease. My gut told me my decision to meet Harper head-on was going to change things. But whether for better or worse, I had no idea.

The snow continued to fall, as if daring me to step out into the unknown. And for the first time in a long while, I was ready to take on the challenge.

CHAPTER 3

Judy

Christmas has always been a season close to my heart, a love affair that started in childhood. The moment Halloween was over, I can't resist to urge to haul out the Christmas decorations from their dusty storage boxes. This year, the early snowfall only fueled my festive spirit, inspiring me to expand my holiday display. With visions of adding new lawn ornaments to my yard dancing in my head, I made a beeline to the hardware store after leaving the bakery, determined to gather everything I needed before the looming storm hit.

The store was bustling with customers scrambling for snow shovels. I chuckled to myself, realizing they were most likely newcomers to the area. Snowfall here was rare, and when it happened, it usually melted by the next day. I could only remember one or two occasions when anyone needed a snow shovel. And when the temperatures stayed below freezing, the beautiful snow would turn to ice—something no shovel could fix.

I skirted past the long line at the checkout. Grabbing a

few small cans of paint, then made my way to the lumber section to pick up a couple of half sheets of plywood and a new aluminum ladder. My old wooden one was heavy and unstable. I was steering my flatbed cart toward the front when a man in a red apron over well-worn blue jeans and a tight-fitting red flannel shirt approached. He reminded me of those sexy Santa Claus pictures you see on social media this time of year.

He gave me a warm smile. "Can I help you?"

"Oh, no thank you. I found everything. I just need to check out."

He stared at my cart. "That must be some project. What kind of car do you have?"

"I have an SUV. I'm sure this will all fit."

He nodded. "Follow me and I'll ring you up."

He led me to the contractor's counter while ignoring the curious looks from the other customers waiting to pay for their shovels.

"Just so you know, we have a delivery service if you ever need it."

"Thank you, I'll remember that." I felt heat rise in my cheeks for some inexplicable reason.

He took a price gun from the cradle and scanned everything. "That will be $64.20."

I pulled the cash from my wallet and handed it to him. He returned my change with a smile that made the corners of his eyes crinkle. Eyes that were an incredible shade of gray with flecks of blue.

"Why don't you go pull your SUV around and I'll load this up for you."

I was still looking into his eyes. I'd never seen eyes that color before. "Uh yes, okay. Thank you."

Fumbling to pull my keys from my coat pocket, I headed out the door. I heard him pushing the cart along behind me.

Pressing a button on my fob lifted the tailgate. With a moving blanket was already in place to protect the carpet. I stood watching while he made quick work of loading my supplies. I became acutely aware of my hands and unsure of what to do with them.

He closed the tailgate. "You're all set."

"Thank you…."

"Nick," He held out his hand.

"Judy." I smiled, shaking his hand. Despite the cold, his hands felt warm and calloused from manual labor.

"Nice to meet you, Judy. Let me know how the project turns out."

A wave of warmth washed over me. "I'll do that," I said, offering another smile, then hastily turned back to my car.

As I pulled away, I glanced in the rearview mirror to see Nick watching me leave. A hazy recollection of seeing him in the store flickered through my mind, but we'd never exchanged words until tonight.

Once home, I waited for the garage door to lift. A single snowflake drifted onto the windshield. I unloaded the supplies, already looking forward to a quiet evening in front of the TV to check the latest weather forecast. My thoughts wandered to Harper and her team, all the dedication they had poured into planning the holiday festival events. I knew that the impending storm would send them into a frenzy, scrambling to prepare a contingency plan.

Settling under a cozy blanket with a cup of tea, I watched the T.V. screen come to life, displaying a bar graph of the week's temperatures. Nighttime lows would dip into the single digits, with the highs hovering just below the thirties until Friday, when they'd finally nudge into the forties. I crossed my fingers for a clear forecast for the parade and the rest of the festival.

Skipping the rest of the news, I headed to the kitchen to

make a grilled cheese and tomato soup, my idea of a perfect dinner on a cold, wintry night. Checking the time. I should have heard from Harper by now. I hoped the storm hadn't caused her any trouble. Reaching for my phone to check in, I realized it wasn't in my pocket. No luck when I checked my coat pockets or the garage. Panic set in. Where had I left it? I scoured the garage, wondering if it had fallen out while I was unloading the supplies from the hardware store.

The hardware store!

I ran back inside and picked up the house phone. I dialed the number listed on my receipt. It rang several times before a man's voice answered.

"Hello?"

"Uh, hello, is this Jansen's Hardware?"

The man didn't respond right away. There was a scraping sound, like he might be moving something heavy.

"Yes, it is. I'm sorry I was in the middle of something. How can I help you?"

"I'm sorry to bother you, but I think I may have left my cell phone in there earlier. Actually, I'm not sure where it is. I seemed to have lost it, and I'm hoping I left it in your store."

"When were you in?"

"A few hours ago, I bought a ladder and some wood."

"Oh yes, I remember you." The man's voice softened. "This is Nick. Listen, I'm in my workshop. I'll walk back through the store and see if I can find it."

"I hate to put you through all that trouble. I was just hoping someone may have seen it and turned it in at the register or something. I can check back in the morning if you are open."

"Won't you need your phone before then?"

"I'm sure I can manage until tomorrow. It's only one night."

"Still, what if the power goes out and your landline doesn't work? I would feel better if I checked the store for it."

"No, please. I can't ask you to do that in this weather. Seriously, I'll be fine until morning."

"It was Judy, right?"

Feeling surprised and flattered that he remembered my name, my cheeks reddened. "Yes, that's right. Nick, please don't spend your time looking for my lost phone. If the weather breaks and you're open tomorrow, I'll come by."

"It is no trouble. My workshop is behind the store."

"Oh, okay, if you're sure it isn't a problem, I really appreciate it."

"Talk to you soon."

"Bye," I whispered, suddenly not wanting to hang up. But the call ended, and I stared at the handset for a moment. What just happened?

I punched in Harper's number.

The phone rang twice. "Mom? Are you okay? I tried calling you," Harper said when she answered the phone.

"Yes, I'm fine, but I seem to have lost my cell phone."

"Oh, no! Do you think you left it at work?"

"I'm sure I had it after leaving the bakery. I stopped by the hardware store so it could be there."

"I'm sorry mom, want me to go look for it?"

"No, it is too late, the weather is too nasty, and it can all wait until tomorrow. I've already called the hardware store and asked them to be on the lookout for it and I'll stop by tomorrow if the roads are clear."

"Do you have your laptop with you, or is that at work?"

"It's in my bag in the other room. But other than making sure you are okay. I'm looking forward to a break from my phone."

"I'm fine mom, I've been home for a while and plan to

work from home tomorrow. But if I need anything, I'll call the house phone."

"Okay, sweetie, that sounds good. I think I'll go curl up with a good book before bedtime."

"Enjoy!"

"Love you."

"Love you too, mom."

Nick's comment about the power replayed in my head, and I thought it couldn't hurt to be prepared. I started a load of laundry as well and made another cup of tea. I loved nights like this. It felt like time froze, leaving me with nothing but a good book.

I must have dozed off while reading, because lights sweeping across the front of the house jolted me awake. Normally I wouldn't have paid any attention to it, but I wondered who would be out on a night like this and this late. I hoped it wasn't Harper.

A knock at the door startled me.

I opened the door to find Nick, from the hardware store, standing there with snowflakes collecting on his shoulders.

"Nick, what are you doing here?"

He held up his hand. "I found your phone in the parking lot of the store, so I brought it over."

"Uh, thank you. How did you know where I lived?"

"You have an 'in case of emergency' note with your home address listed. I saw it when I picked up the phone and checked to see if it was yours. You really should password protect your phone, by the way." He as he handed it to me.

Yeah, you're right, but I find it inconvenient to tap out a password because my hands are usually covered in flour or dough.

He gave me a curious look. "Dough?"

"I'm a baker." I held up my hands.

"Right." He didn't look convinced and took a step back. "Well, I should be going."

A stronger need for him to stay overrode my nervousness that he had found my house. "Wait, you drove all the way here. That couldn't have been easy in this weather. Let me offer you coffee or tea to warm you up a bit." I stepped aside to allow him to come in.

"I don't want to inconvenience you. And besides, I have a four-wheel-drive truck that can get through just about anything. I just thought in a storm you might need your phone." He spoke the words, but he didn't move.

"At least let me give you a cup of coffee to go."

"Okay." He stomped the snow off his boots and stepped inside.

I closed the door against the cold. "Follow me."

"Wow, this is an impressive kitchen." He said, looking around as I took coffee from the cabinet.

"I wasn't kidding when I said I was a baker."

"I guess not." He said with an appreciative smile.

"Do you prefer coffee, tea, or cocoa?"

"Hot cocoa?" He grinned.

"You got it." I smiled and put the coffee back and brought out the chocolate. "I own and operate Baby Cakes Bakery."

"I love that place!"

"Really? I don't recall ever seeing you in there." I was sure I would remember if I had.

"I think I've only been one or twice, but Tricia, one of my employees, brings baked goods to work from your place regularly and always brings someone a cupcake on their birthday."

"That is a sweet thing to do. Please, let me take your coat."

"Thank you." He peeled off his coat to reveal the same snug fitting red flannel shirt he had been wearing earlier. I tried to think of something other than him in a sexy Santa suit.

"Tricia has a heart of gold." He added.

I hung his coat on a peg by the back door. "Please have a seat, anywhere."

He chose a stool at the breakfast bar, which was close to the stove where I warmed the milk. Once prepared, I poured it into a festive mug and swiftly placed a cupcake from under the glass cover onto a plate before serving it to him.

"Wow!"

"The cupcake is chocolate with peanut butter icing."

He stared at it and removed the paper, taking a bite. "That is delicious!" he mumbled with a mouthful.

"I'm glad you like it."

"It is fantastic." He took another bite and a sip of cocoa. "I am going to be wired all night."

Laughing, I asked, "That isn't such a bad thing, is it? I mean, you wouldn't want to miss our one snowfall of the year."

"You're right. All of this panic and it will probably all be gone tomorrow."

CHAPTER 4

Harper

December 2nd

I woke up early. The unusual way light shone through the window was making it hard to stay asleep. I padded into the living room, opening the curtain to peer outside. I couldn't believe my eyes. Sliding open the glass door, and reached out, half-expecting to wake from a dream. Snow piled high on my balcony, rekindling the childhood thrill of a snow day. But the feeling was short-lived, and I knew this snowfall would cast a shadow over the holiday celebrations.

Now that I was awake, I needed coffee. Just as I scooped some into the filter basket, the power went out.

"Dammit!" I rushed back to the sliding glass doors. It appeared to be a widespread power outage. All the lights on the street trees were out and the few lights I had seen on in other buildings just moments ago were gone, too.

My cell phone rang. "Hello?"

"Harper, it's mom, you, okay?"

"Hi mom, I'm okay. Do you have power?"

"Yes, why? Don't you?"

I sighed, "No, it just went out."

"Oh, no!"

I sank down onto the sofa. "Yeah, it went out before I had my coffee and a shower."

"Why don't you come over here?"

"Mom, have you seen the snow outside? There has to be six inches of snow out on the ground. You know I can't drive in this mess."

"I guess you have a point. Hang on a minute." My mother's voice sounded further away from the phone. "My daughter lives in the central district. They lost power."

"Mom, who are you talking to?"

"Just a minute, dear."

I waited. The phone was silent, suggesting that my mother had put me on hold.

"Hello, Harper. If you want to come over, my friend Nick can pick you up and bring you over here? He has four-wheel drive."

"Mom, who is Nick? You've never mentioned anyone named Nick before."

"It's a long story. Do you want Nick to come get you?"

"Is it safe?" I was torn. I wanted to say no, but now I was worried that my mother was in her house alone with a man I didn't know.

"Well, if it wasn't, I'm sure he wouldn't offer."

"I don't know, mom, it is a longer drive from your house to the office if I need to go in. But I'm concerned that you are alone with a stranger."

"Harper Renee, what kind of woman do you think I am?"

"I mean no disrespect, mom, but I am worried. How well do you know this man?"

"Well, enough to trust him with my only daughter."

I guess she had a point.

"I'll tough it out here for a while. Hopefully, it will be back on shortly."

"Ok, call me if you need anything."

"You, too."

We hung up, and I called Christina.

"Hello?" Christina's voice sounded groggy, like she was sleeping.

"Christina, are you still in bed?" I demanded.

"Yeah, snow day."

"I know it's a snow day, but I have a crisis on my hands."

Christina yawned. "I'm sure they will still have Christmas."

"I'm not talking about Christmas or work. My mother is alone with some man named Nick!"

"What?" Christina sounded more alert and with the appropriate amount of shock in her voice. "Nick Tanner?"

"Who is Nick Tanner?"

"You know Nick, he runs Jansen Hardware."

I paused, trying to picture the employees any time I went into the hardware store, which, I must admit, wasn't often.

Christina waited, "Nothing?"

"No, I can't picture him."

"You're hopeless, but good for your mom because Nick is hot as hell, even for a guy your mom's age."

"Ew, don't say things like that. I don't want to think about my mother and some hot guy."

Christina laughed, "Where do you think you came from, an egg?"

"I know, I know. But it kinda freaks me out a little to

think about my mom dating again. I need a minute to wrap my head around it."

"Harper, I know you want your mom to be happy."

"Of course I do. I also know there are a lot of creeps out there ready to take advantage of a trusting person like mom. I don't want one of them taking advantage of her."

"I can understand that, but I know, Nick. He's a wonderful guy. I think if you met him, you wouldn't worry so much."

I sighed. "Perhaps you're right. I have a lot on my mind right now and I don't need one more thing to worry about."

"I understand, but your mom raised three kids and runs her own business. I think she can handle dating."

"I hope you're right."

"So, since you woke me up, I assume you're trying to work from home?"

"Well, I was going to until the power went out. In fact, I should probably go. I might need to conserve my phone's battery."

"Yes, you should! You don't want to have an emergency and not be able to call anyone."

"Okay, I'll talk to you later."

"Love you like a sis."

"Same!" I hung up and thought about what Christina had said. My mother deserved to be happy.

I went back to the kitchen to check for milk.

As I ate my cold cereal, I admired the snow outside, hoping it might linger long enough for a white Christmas—though, knowing our luck, it would be sixty degrees by then. I pulled out my laptop and started sifting through emails. A Plan B was in order for the tree lighting ceremony; Several messages confirmed city offices were closed, including one from my boss suggesting we postpone the event by a week. Perfect. I hoped a week would give the work crews enough time to clear the streets and the park where the tree lighting would be held. And while I would love a white Christmas, I hoped the snow would melt in a few days and we would have better conditions for the parade and tree lighting.

I replied to my boss, offering to post the update on the website, and reached out to the communications team to help spread the word. Additionally, I provided a quick synopsis of the budget meeting from the day before and suggested that a change in plans may also change our staffing needs. I hated bypassing Daniel, knowing my director would involve the city manager if needed, but there was no other option. I' make sure I fought harder for an increase in our budget for next year.

With that settled, it was easier to relax, though the need for a cup of coffee lingered. Regret crept in about turning down the mother's invitation. Surely, someone nearby had coffee. Bundling up in my warmest clothes, I headed downstairs and venture out into the winter wonderland.

Once out on the sidewalk, I glanced up and down the street. I hated to mess up the pristine snow with my footprints, but the desire for coffee was strong and I trekked up the street to see if any of the usual cafes or restaurants were open. After four blocks, I found a coffee shop open next to the park. It boasted a walk-up window for those days when people were enjoying the weather.

I was relieved to find a few other people were out enjoying the snow.

"Large coffee, black." Stamping my feet to keep them warm. "Please."

The man smiled and poured me a cup, adding a lid for me. "Here you go. That will be $1.75."

As I handed over the money, I thought I would have willingly paid him $50 at this point. "Thank you, you are a lifesaver."

He smiled again. "Cold morning for a walk."

"My apartment doesn't have power. I walked four blocks looking for coffee before I found you. Thank you for being here."

"No power? Come back before you walk back home. I'll give you a warm up."

"Thank you." Sipping the coffee, I stepped away to watch some kids have a snowball fight. Closing my eyes for a moment, I enjoyed the warmth of the coffee, knowing it might be my last for a while. I took out my phone and checked the battery level, wondering if I should risk calling the power company's eight hundred number for an estimate on when power would be restored.

Taking off my glove, I tapped the number on the screen. A recorded message announced that power restoration could take anywhere from twenty-four to forty-eight hours. I ended the call and stared up at the sky. The clouds offered no hope of warmth today. I sighed and turned back towards the coffee shop for a refill before heading home.

"Harper?"

Turning toward the person calling my name, I saw him. Daniel was walking towards me. I steeled myself for whatever he was going to say, probably something about not asking for more money for the event, considering the storm.

"Hi, Daniel."

"I didn't know you lived near here." He said.

"I live four blocks that way, but my building is out of power and so I came in search of coffee."

"Oh, I'm sorry, any idea how long the power will be out?"

I held up my phone. "Couple of days."

"You can't stay in your apartment for a couple of days with no heat."

"I hadn't thought about that problem yet. My priority was getting coffee."

He chuckled, and I thought I could almost like him. He was dressed for jogging.

"Why are you jogging in the snow? Seems like that could be dangerous."

"It could be, I suppose. But I have to run every day, and the cold and snow don't bother me."

Unsure of what else to say, I nodded in agreement. "Well, I won't keep you any longer."

"You can't go back home with no heat. Do you have someplace else you can go?" He asked.

"My mother invited me to her house, but she lives on the west side of town and the roads are too bad."

"My place isn't far. You're welcome to come over," he offered. I stared at him, speechless. Noticing my reaction, he backpedaled, a flush creeping up his neck. "That... didn't come out right. I didn't mean to imply—"

"Thank you, but I couldn't impose," I stammered out. My mind raced, trying to reconcile this unexpected kindness with our usual work dynamic of butting heads.

"I would feel bad knowing you walked home in the snow to a cold apartment with no heat and no way to cook. Please, come over and at least warm up and have lunch with me."

I was surprised by how quickly he offered to help me. Frankly, I was shocked that he even stopped to say hello. I had to admit I wasn't always as nice as I could be to him and here he was offering to help me. I felt embarrassed for my past attitude towards him.

"I wouldn't refuse a chance to charge up my cell phone." I replied.

"Come on, I'll drive you to your place and you grab your laptop or anything else you need, and you can charge up your stuff and warm up."

"You drove here? How? The streets are a mess."

"The trucks are out, and I followed a snowplow here. And my car has all-wheel drive."

"Wow, I'm impressed they are out already."

"Well, at least on the major streets."

Once again I felt embarrassed about the things I had thought about him before today. I followed him to his car and held my breath as he navigated the unplowed streets. Daniel parked in front of my building, and I ran upstairs and grabbed a change of clothes and my laptop and work cell phone.

CHAPTER 5

Harper

Daniel skillfully navigated the snowy streets on the way back to his house, which turned out to be a beautiful, old Victorian.

"This place is amazing," I said, looking at the leaded glass windows.

"Thank you, it needed a lot of TLC when I bought it but, I got it at a steal. I've been restoring it for a couple of years."

I don't know why I was surprised, but I was in awe of Daniel's handiness. "You've done all this yourself?"

"Most of it, some things I leave to the experts, like the rewiring." He smiled and took my coat. "Would you like more coffee or hot chocolate?"

"I think I should slow down on the caffeine for a while."

Daniel nodded, "two waters coming up. Please have a seat. Make yourself at home."

The awkwardness crept over me like a cold mist, settling

into my bones. I shifted my weight from one foot to the other, my awareness of every movement intensified.

A memory flashed through my mind - Daniel fervently explaining his viewpoint in a meeting, and me internally rolling my eyes. The recollection made me wince. This wasn't me. I wasn't the type to hastily dismiss others, to build walls without reason.

"Is everything okay?" Daniel asked, his brow furrowing with concern.

His gentle tone pierced through my self-recrimination. Why had I been so harsh towards him? He seemed to know my deepest secrets, guilt crushing my conscience. I'd crafted a villain in my mind, and now that imaginary foe was crumbling before my eyes, leaving only a man - kind, awkward, and not at all the villain I had constructed in my mind.

"I'm fine," I lied, forcing a smile. But inside, a voice whispered, demanding answers I wasn't sure I was ready to face.

Daniel nodded and disappeared into a kitchen down the hall. Taking the opportunity to reexamine myself, I was ashamed of my past behavior. I had no valid justification for it. I scanned the photos on the fireplace mantel; pictures of Daniel as a boy with a dog, another with him, and a little girl. I presumed to be his sister.

Daniel returned and handed me a bottled water. I needed to be more open-minded. "Did you grow up here?" Suddenly wanting to know more about him.

"Yes," he nodded.

"How did you learn to drive in the snow?"

He laughed, putting the top back on his water. "I went to school in Pennsylvania. It's the perfect place to learn."

"Oh, I knew it couldn't have been here."

"Don't you like the snow?"

"I love it. I just can't drive in it."

"We don't get much practice around here, that's for sure,"

he chuckled, "but I got plenty of practice in Philadelphia." He gave me a warm smile, and I wondered why I never realized he had a charming smile.

"Uh, Daniel, can I say something?" I felt like I had to apologize. The awkwardness was killing me.

"Sure." He furrowed his brow.

"I feel like I should apologize to you for all the budget stuff."

He gazed at me for a moment, his eyes softened. "No need, I understand. It's work. It's the way it is."

"I know, but I didn't mean to give you such a hard time, and I wasn't blaming you personally....,"

He held up his hand. "It's okay. I know I am not always the popular guy at work. Trust me, I hate telling you and others no. I wish we could fund everything."

The sincerity in his eyes made me feel even worse. "Thank you, you're too kind."

He smiled. "Don't worry about it. Okay?" He paused as if waiting for me to agree.

Smiling back at him, I nodded. "Okay."

"Excellent. Now, what can I get you? You must be hungry."

"Oh goodness, no. I can't have you feeding me too. You've been so kind already."

"Harper, seriously, you can't sit here all day and not eat."

On que my stomach rumbled, giving me away.

"Do you absolutely need to work? I mean right now?" He asked.

"No, I don't suppose not. We've put out update to the website and sent emails postponing the tree lighting until next week. Not much else I can do at the moment."

"Awesome!" He stood up, taking me by surprise. "How do you feel about grilled cheese sandwiches, tomato soup, and hot cocoa?"

I beamed. "Sounds like all the comfort foods of my childhood."

"And this is probably a dumb question but, do you like Christmas movies?"

I giggled, not knowing why, "Yeah."

"I vote for watching a Christmas movie marathon with all our favorite comfort foods and let the world deal with the winter wonderland outside!" He beamed.

"You've got a deal!" I couldn't resist an offer like that, and it had been ages since I did nothing for a whole day. "What can I do to help?"

"How are you with cocoa?"

"I can handle that."

"Okay, you're team cocoa, and I am team soup and sandwiches."

Following him to the kitchen, he showed me where he kept all the coca supplies, and I set us up a little hot cocoa bar with whipped cream and cinnamon while he heated canned tomato soup and made the sandwiches.

I studied him masterfully, juggle everything. "You've done this before." I said.

"Once or twice." He grinned.

Once again, I was surprised that my opinions of him were incorrect. Based on our budget meetings, I would have thought he was more of the scrooge type.

When everything was ready, we carried trays of food and drink into the living room and settled on the sofa. Daniel grabbed the remote and turned on the TV.

"Oh, I almost forget!" He went over to an old shipping trunk sitting in the corner. It had a weathered look to it, the brass fittings tarnished to a rich patina. The scratches and scuffs held the secrets of travel from days long past. Daniel lifted the heavy lid and pulled out a large blanket. "Do you want to share, or do you want your own?"

Sensing my hesitation, he added, "It's extra-large, but I've got plenty, if you prefer."

"No, we can share." I smiled. We are adults, and I'm not a prude.

He nodded and brought over a large, soft, gray blanket. It was undeniably enormous. You could have fit four people under it.

We got under the blanket and grabbed our trays of soup and sandwiches. Daniel pulled up a list of Christmas movies. "What's your favorite?"

I scanned the list. "Miracle on 34th Street, the original."

"Excellent choice." With a click of the remote, the movie started.

By the time the movie ended, I was warm, toasty, and starting to feel sleepy. Daniel had already dozed off. I told myself I could close my eyes for just a minute.

When my eyes fluttered open, I found myself in unfamiliar surroundings. The first thing I noticed was the unexpected weight across my body—a blanket tucked under my chin. Blinking away the remnants of sleep, I tried to place where I was. The large TV on the wall was much bigger than mine, and the room didn't look familiar. Then I spotted the shipping trunk in the corner, and memories of Daniel came rushing back. As if on cue, the front door opened.

"Oh hey, I hope I didn't wake you."

"I'm so sorry. I didn't mean to fall asleep like that."

"Don't worry about it. I wanted to shovel the walk while it was still light enough to see what I was doing."

"Oh, let me help you."

Daniel put his hand up, "No, you are a guest and besides, it's done."

"I feel like I should help."

"You made some excellent cocoa, and you are wonderful company on a cold winter's day."

"Some company."

"I'll take it as a compliment that you felt comfortable enough to fall asleep."

He had a point. I smoothed my hair and glanced around the room. "What time is it?" Looking around for my phone.

"It's about two o'clock."

"Really? I should check on my mom."

"Please," he said, indicating I should relax on the sofa. "Would you like something else to drink?"

Feeling self-conscious about how I must look, I tucked a strand of hair behind my ear. "No, thank you. I'm fine right now."

He nodded and walked into the kitchen, giving me some privacy. I dialed my mother's number.

"Hello, Harper?"

"Hi mom, checking in to make sure you are okay."

"Oh yes, I'm fine. I'm baking chocolate chip cookies for dessert later. Do you want me to pick you up so you can come for dinner?"

"No, actually, I'm at a friend's house."

"Oh good, I was going to ask if you had power yet."

"Not yet. Power company says it might take twenty-four to forty-eight hours."

"Well, why don't you and your friend come for dinner?"

"I'd love to mom, I'll ask him and text you, okay?"

"Him?"

"Mom, don't start."

She laughed, "Okay, but bring him for dinner."

"I'll text you. Bye." Daniel walked in as I ended the call.

"Everything okay?"

"Oh yeah, she is baking chocolate chip cookies and invited us both for dinner later." I fidgeted with the phone in my hand, hoping he would say yes, and also terrified at the same time.

"Is she a good cook?" He asked jokingly.

"Oh yeah. I'd say so. She owns Baby Cakes Bakery."

"Judy is your mom?" He asked with a shocked expression on his face.

Equally surprised, I asked, "How do you know my mom?"

"I have a coffee and croissant from the bakery every morning."

I was fascinated and a little upset that my mother had been consorting with the enemy this whole time and never said a word. Then I remembered he wasn't the enemy. He invited me into his home.

"I better text her back and tell her we'll be joining her for dinner." I smiled.

"Are you sure?" he asked, understanding my nervousness.

I strived to recover quickly. "Absolutely, I mean, if you don't mind driving." I have him a devilish grin.

He relaxed, "I don't mind. Not for a meal and dessert prepared by your mom!"

I had to laugh; she has a very loyal customer base.

He settled himself on the sofa next to me. "What time is dinner? Do you think we have time for one more movie?"

I tried not to think about how weird this day and turned out. "I think we do."

"What'll be?"

"You pick this time."

"Okay…."Picking up the remote, he flipped through the movie titles.

He stopped on Lethal Weapon.

"How is this a Christmas movie?"

"You'll see." He wiggled his eyebrows up and down.

I sighed and pulled the blanket over me.

Despite the lack of feel-good Christmas cheer, I enjoyed the movie.

"What did you think?" He asked when it was over.

"It was good, but I think calling it a Christmas movie is still a stretch."

He laughed, "We can agree to disagree. We're good at that."

I laughed with him embarrassment creeping up again. "I guess you're right."

"Shall we go to dinner?" He asked, holding out his arm.

"Lets." I took his arm in dramatic fashion as he walked me to the door.

He navigated us to my mother's house with no problems. I noticed a pickup truck parked in the driveway that I didn't recognize. Daniel parked the car and caught me staring at the truck. "Something wrong?"

"I don't recognize that truck."

He studied it for a minute. "That has to be Nick's truck. Does your mom know Nick Tanner?"

I turned to him. "How come everyone knows this Nick Tanner but me?"

"I don't know," he shrugged, "but he's a cool guy."

"Hmpf," I said, feeling like I was suddenly out of the loop. The sidewalk and driveway had been cleared, and I wondered if the wonderful Nick Tanner was responsible.

I walked in my mother's front door. "Hello?"

Mom appeared from the kitchen, wearing her apron. "Harper! I'm so glad you made it!" She rushed over to hug me. "Have you eaten? Are you frozen?"

I smiled, "I'm fine, mom. This is Daniel. We work together."

She turned her attention to him. "Hi Daniel, it's so good to see you. I'm sorry I wasn't open for your morning coffee and croissant." She smiled.

Daniel smiled. "I totally understand. Thank you for having me over. You have a beautiful home."

My mother blushed a little. "Thank you. That is sweet,

and you are always welcome for dinner. Any friend of Harper's." The timer went off in the kitchen. "Excuse me." She dashed out of sight.

"Let me take your things." I offered Daniel. He reached to help me with my coat. I was marveling at how different he seemed outside of work. While turning back to take his coat, I heard a baritone voice emanating from the kitchen. I fought the urge to charge in and demand to know who he was and what he would be doing in my mother's house.

"Ut oh," Daniel said as I faced the hallway leading to the kitchen.

"What?"

"I know that look."

"What look?"

"The look that says you are on the warpath." His mouth twitched at the corners.

"It does not." I frowned.

He held up his hands in surrender. "Okay."

I walked past him to the kitchen, to find a man, correction a handsome man with thick silver and black hair, and a strong jawline. Despite the rugged good looks, it was his eyes that held my attention. I couldn't stop looking at him.

"…. I adjusted the flame on the furnace. It should run more efficiently now."

My mother gave him a warm smile that I didn't like. "Thank you. You didn't have to do that. Please let me pay you."

"No, no. It was no problem. I can't take your money."

"How about a warm cookie?" She laughed. I threw up a little in my mouth.

"Mom?"

She turned to me as Mr. Silver Haired Fox accepted the cookie and took a bite. "What is it, darling?" She said in a voice that sounded sweet to everyone else, but I knew the tone. It was her annoyed tone. The one that said I will deal with you later, not in front of guests.

Daniel blurted out, "Nick! What are you doing here?"

I eyed both Daniel and Nick.

"Hey, buddy!" Nick crossed the kitchen in two strides. "I could ask you the same thing." The two men shook hands.

"You two know each other?" My mother and I said in unison.

Nick was the first to speak. "Daniel single handedly keeps me in business with all of his home renovations and repairs."

"Plus, Nick and I are both football fans."

Nick nodded. "Guess we'll have to postpone the party this weekend."

"You think so?" Daniel asked.

With the two of them immersed in a conversation about a football party, I stepped closer to my mother and whisper. "What is he doing here?"

"I told you; I dropped my phone, and he brought it to me."

Clenching my teeth to keep my voice down. "That was last night. Is there anything you want to tell me?"

"No, dear."

"No, you don't want to tell me?" I tried again.

"Is that the same Daniel you've been complaining about for ages?"

"That is not important right now," I hissed.

My mother laughed, catching the attention of Nick and Daniel. The two men paused and refocused on us. Nick smiled a charming smile that no doubt worked on women of a certain age, like my mother.

He held out his hand. "Hello, I'm Nick Tanner."

"Harper, Judy's daughter."

"Yes, I see the family resemblance."

My mother tucked a piece of hair behind her ear, and I resisted the urge to roll my eyes. I shook Nick's hand. "A pleasure to meet you. Do you live close by?" I asked sweetly, but I could feel my mother's eyes on me.

"Not too far."

"Hmm," I nodded.

Before I could ask any more questions, my mother steered the men into the den. "If you two want to turn on a game or something, please feel free. Harper is going to help me with dinner."

"Mom, I'm sure Nick must have some snow shovels to sell or something."

My mother pinched my arm, and I tried not to squeal. "Nick is invited to dinner, so everyone might as well relax and enjoy yourselves."

Nick and Daniel stood frozen, looking at the two of us. "Well, go on." My mother shooed them into the den. "You'll be underfoot in the kitchen."

For a minute, I thought Nick might leave, but he and Daniel sat down and clicked on the TV. My mother grabbed my arm and drug me out of earshot. "What has gotten into you?"

"Me? What has gotten into you? Inviting a stranger over for dinner?"

"Nick is not a stranger. I shop at the hardware store all the time; you know that."

"Well, I would think you would be a little more careful about who you bring home." My temper was flashing.

"I didn't bring him home, as you say, and I do not like your tone, young lady, and don't think I won't send you up to your room until dinner is ready."

"Don't think I won't go!"

"Is everything alright?" Nick asked from the doorway.

I frowned at him.

"We are having a mother and daughter moment." My mother forced a smile.

"Perhaps I should go," He offered.

"You will do no such thing." My mother put her hands on her hips and in this house, that meant things were about to go from bad to worse. Wooden spoons at fifty paces were a real possibility.

"I studied my mother with interest while she tried to hide her embarrassment; I could feel the guilt creeping up my spine."

"Please stay," I said. "I apologize. It has been a stressful couple of weeks, and I think this snow and lack of power at my apartment has me on edge."

Nick smiled. "I can understand." He turned and went back to the den.

My mother glared at me and went about pulling ingredients from the fridge and the cabinets. I stood for a moment, feeling ashamed of myself before offering to help.

CHAPTER 6

❄

Harper

Seeing an extra place at the table. "Who's the extra place setting for, mom?" I asked, carrying in the taurine of peas and onions.

"I invited Christina earlier in the day. I'm not sure if she will make it through."

As if on cue, the front door opened and Christina called from the foyer, "I'm here, I'm here!"

She rushed into the dining room, her eyes widening as they landed on Daniel and Nick.

"Oh!" The word escaped her lips in a soft gasp. A rosy flush crept up her neck, coloring her cheeks. "I didn't realize... I mean, I'm so sorry for keeping you waiting." Visibly flustered, she smoothed her hair and straightened her back.

I watched with amusement as Mom hugged her. "Glad you could make it. I was getting worried."

"Well, I wish I had a valid excuse, but I don't, other than it took me longer than I thought it would to drive over here in the snow."

"You should have called. One of us would've come and picked you up." Nick smiled at her.

Christina gave him a bright smile. "I thought Judy would have you out back chopping wood for the fireplace or something."

Nick chuckled, "I already did that."

"He did not!" My mom argued, putting her hands on her hips.

I walked over and hugged her, then turned in the direction of Daniel. "Christina, this is Daniel Stewart, a friend of mine from work."

"A pleasure to meet you," Christina held out her hand. "I'm Christina Keats, Harper's best friend."

"Truly? I bet you have the inside track on Harper." Daniel joked.

"Oh, the stories I could tell." Christina laughed.

"But she won't." I grumped.

My mother broke the tension, "If everyone would like to be seated, I think dinner is getting cold."

We all ate quietly, and I knew it irritated my mother. Mom enjoyed a good dinner conversation.

"So, Daniel, Nick said you are renovating a house?" My mother asked when she couldn't take the silence any longer.

"Yes, I bought an old Victorian on River Road and have spent the past couple of years restoring it."

"How wonderful. The homes are lovely in that neighborhood." She smiled and surveyed the table, expecting the rest of us to agree with her. We all nodded and smiled.

Nick picked up on the conversation. "I keep telling him to document the transformation. He could put it up on social media or something."

"Oh, you'd have tons of followers." Christina added.

"Yeah, I'm not sure that is my thing. Working on the house helps me relax. Posting it might take away the fun part."

My mother's gaze fell on me. "What do you think, Harper?"

"I think Daniel's house is gorgeous and I agree with him it is private, and it would make it less special if half the world was watching him during his downtime."

Daniel gave me a grateful smile. My mother frowned.

Christina eyed me suspiciously. "How do you know his house is gorgeous?"

I answered her with what I hoped was a terrifying look. "Because Daniel was kind enough to let me hang out at his place today, since my apartment is going to be out of power for a couple of days."

My mother and Christina both gaped at me before they both snapped out of it. Nick kept his face neutral, but glanced over at Daniel. He earned a few points in the respect department at that moment. I thought he must have an awesome poker face.

"That was kind of you, Daniel. I'm sure Harper spent her time working on her laptop."

"Actually,"

I bumped Daniel under the table.

"She did. It is amazing how much work she has to do, even when the city is closed."

My respect for him went up about ten points at that moment. My mother took a bite of her chicken. Before commenting further. I gave Daniel a quick grin of thanks.

Thankfully, the meal ended. "Mom, why don't you relax, and Christina and I will do the dishes," I offered.

Daniel diverted Mom's attention from me. "I'd love to hear more about what Harper was like as a little girl."

I wasn't sure whether or not to feel grateful, but I knew I could survive Mom showing him pictures of me in a Girl Scout uniform or that time I caught a fish on a camping trip. At least I had a few minutes alone with Christina.

Once we were alone, Christina leaned in and whispered, "What the hell is going on with you today?"

"Me? What is going on with my mom? Why is there a stranger at the dinner table that apparently has been here all day?"

"Nick is not a stranger."

"I don't like him."

"Why?"

"I don't know, I just don't."

Christina stared at me. "Okay, so you don't like the idea of your mom dating, and besides, I thought we talked about this today."

"I do want her to be happy and yes, we talked about it."

"So, what's the problem?"

"I don't know." I snapped.

"What is up with you and Daniel? You hung out at his house today? How well do you know him?"

"And I told you, we work together." I dried a plate within an inch of its life.

"That isn't the same Daniel from the budget office, is it?"

I didn't answer her right away.

"Harper, it is him, isn't it? Oh, I need to hear this!"

I glanced over my shoulder to see if anyone was listening. "I may have been mistaken about him."

"May have?"

"Okay, I admit it; I was wrong. This morning, I went out to find coffee while he went out for a jog. Surprisingly, we bumped into each other in a park."

"Jogging in this weather?"

"That is what I said."

Christina did a quick check over her shoulder. "So, how did you end up at his house?"

"He invited me after I told him my power was out."

"Wow, that was sweet of him."

"Yes." I started drying the silverware while Christina went to work on the glassware.

"So, did you actually work on your laptop all day?"

"No, I didn't. We made grilled cheese sandwiches, hot cocoa and watched Christmas movies."

"Geeze, I think I've been replaced."

I laughed, "You're ridiculous."

"You girls almost finished?" My mom called out.

Christina and I joined my mother, who was sitting with Nick and Daniel on the sofa, a photo album in her lap. The irony of our situation wasn't lost on me. Mother invited Nick into her home on a cold winter's night because he was kind enough to brave the weather to return her lost phone and Daniel had invited me into his home out of pity for my lack of power at my apartment.

"We have. Have you finished humiliating me yet in front of Nick and Daniel?"

"You have nothing to be ashamed of. Harper, you were an adorable child."

Christina leaned in, "Noticed she said nothing about you being an adorable adult."

"I heard that young lady and don't forget I have pictures of you too," my mother threatened.

"Don't forget, I have quite a few of you as well," I countered. "A certain Halloween costume comes to mind."

My mother snapped the photo album shut. "Gentlemen, I think we've seen enough pictures for one night, don't you?" She didn't wait for an answer. "It's time for dessert. Would anyone like to watch a Christmas movie?"

"As long as we are all in agreement about what a

Christmas movie is," I said, giving Daniel a sly look. He tried to hide a grin.

"Everyone loves White Christmas, don't they?" My mom asked.

We all nodded, although I'm not sure that Nick and Daniel would have chosen a musical.

"Who wants to help me with the dessert?"

"I will," Nick said.

I rolled my eyes at Christina. She, Daniel and I went to settle on the sofa in front of the TV, like the three of us had always been friends. I got out the warm blanket while Nick carried a tray with a picture of milk and glasses and my mom brought an enormous plate of chocolate chip and iced Christmas cookies.

Nick and my mom sat in separate overstuffed chairs and my mom brought up the movie on the TV screen. I ate two chocolate chip cookies and one iced cookie. Daniel had two of each and Christina, always in full control, ate one iced cookie.

I was so full after dinner and too many cookies; I was feeling sleepy. The next thing I knew, the movie had ended.

"They don't make movies like that anymore," mom said, standing up and stretching.

"I should go home before it gets too late," Christina said.

"Me too," Nick agreed.

"All of you can stay here. There is no need to drive." Mom offered.

Nick moved towards the front door.

"That is a kind offer, but I need to go. I need to check on the store, even try to open up tomorrow if I can. I'll let you know how the roads are and if they are still bad, I'll come by and pick you up if you want to go into the bakery."

"Thanks, it is kind of you. Yes, please let me know about

the roads." She turned to me. "Harper, you're staying, aren't you? You can't go home to an apartment with no power."

She had a point, and I couldn't very well stay with Daniel.

"If you don't mind, mom, or I could stay with Christina."

"Don't be ridiculous. Of course, you're staying here until your power comes back on."

I sighed. Christina came over and hugged me. Whispering in my ear, she said, "I'll text you later." Nodding, I hugged her.

"Daniel, I'll walk you out," I said, handing him his coat and scarf. He said his goodbyes to my mother, and we stepped outside, leaving my mother alone with Nick.

Christina went to start her car and let it warm up.

When we were alone, I turned to Daniel.

"Thank you for everything today. I feel bad about you driving back alone. Are you sure you will be alright? You can stay."

He glanced back at the house. "As much as I love your mother's cooking and your mother, I'd better go. I can't eat like that all the time." He gave me a sweet smile.

I felt awkward, like that moment on a first date when you don't know if you are supposed to kiss the boy goodnight or not. I took his hand and squeezed it. "Today was fun."

"Yeah?"

I nodded. "Yeah, it was. I loved watching movies and drinking hot cocoa."

Daniel stared at the house, then the ground, pretty much everywhere but at me. Finally, he said, "Can I call you later?"

"Sure! Here, give me your phone." He handed me the phone, and I gave him mine. We each entered our numbers.

He looked down at his phone and smiled and nodded.

"Go inside Harper, before you freeze."

"Okay, text me as soon as you are home, so I know you're safe."

"I will." Daniel got in his car and started the engine. He and Christina each pulled away from the curb. I was wondering if I should go back inside, and I didn't want to think about my mom potentially kissing Nick. But the door opened, and Nick stepped out on to the porch.

"It was wonderful to meet you, Harper."

I have him my best steely stare, but still shook his hand. "You, too. Be careful driving."

"I will. "Nick stepped off the porch and climbed into his truck. My mother was watching from the window.

I had to admit one thing. Nick Tanner was good looking.

Closing the door behind me and shivering as the warmth welcomed me back into the house.

Mom and I stared at one another, and she asked, "What the hell is going on with you?"

"Me?" I asked.

"What are you talking about?" My mother put her hands on her hips.

I stared at her. "You first."

"Okay, first young lady. I don't have to explain anything to you. I am your mother. Second, I didn't raise you to be rude."

"I wasn't rude to anyone and yes, you are my mother, and I can worry about you if I want to. Why would you let a stranger into this house?"

"This is my house, and Nick is not a stranger."

"How long have you known him?"

"Years. He's worked at the hardware store for years."

I narrowed my gaze. "Mom, how long have you known his name?"

She glanced away, and I knew I had her.

"Well?" I crossed my arms over my chest.

"Yesterday."

"Yesterday!"

"Yes, I got some project supplies, and he helped me load it into the SUV and then when I lost my phone, he found it and brought it over to me. Which was quite chivalrous."

"Or stalkerish."

"What? Nick is not a stalker."

"And so why did he come back today?"

My mother got a strange look on her face and walked into the living room. "I don't appreciate your tone."

"Mom, why did he come back? Did he hurt you? Did he try anything with you?" Fear was creeping up my spine. "Mom, you can tell me. Did he try anything funny? Did he put his hands on you?"

"Harper, I don't want to talk about it."

"Oh, my god! Mom, seriously, did he touch you?" I was pulling my phone from my pocket as I spoke, ready to dial 911 and have him arrested.

"Harper!"

"Mom, this is serious. You can't let him get away with it and I can't believe you didn't tell me, and we sat here with him at the dinner table. I will kill him myself with my bare hands!"

"Stop it! Stop it!" My mom yelled. My mother never yelled, not even when we were kids.

Softening my voice. "I'm sorry. I can't stand the thought of you being hurt."

"Harper, honey, it's not like that."

"Then what is it like?"

"Nick didn't leave last night. He stayed over. And before you call the police, I invited him to stay."

"Mother!" I'm not sure which upset me more at the moment. My mother had invited a man to spend the night. My life was turning upside down, and I had no way of stopping it. "What are you talking about?"

"Oh Harper, it's the 21st century! Nothing happened. We

stayed up most of the night talking and he fell asleep on the sofa."

"I can't believe this!" I shook my head, trying to wake myself from whatever bizarre world I was dreaming about, where I was friends with Daniel and my mother was dating Nick, the hardware dude.

CHAPTER 7

Harper

Feeling guilty about my behavior towards mom, I went upstairs to my room to put some distance between us. I needed to catch up on a little work for the holiday festival, anyway. I sat on the edge of my bed thinking about the past twenty-four hours. Being the only sibling that still lived close to mom, I felt extra protective of her. I wanted her to have all the happiness in the world. God knows she deserved it, but I was protective of her, too.

Before checking the weather forecast and my emails. I did a little online research into Nick Tanner. If he was going to be dating my mom, I wanted to know more about him.

All I could find was that he served in the military and was a nice guy, donating time and toys to the children's hospital. I sighed with relief. Now I needed to come up with a firm plan on how to pull off this lighting ceremony that would kick off the holiday festival. Even with the parade and lighting being delayed a week, I still needed to make sure we were ready. The entire team of city staff and I had spent a lot of time and money on this event. Failure was not an option.

I sent out a request for an online meeting with the team for the following day. We needed to regroup and make sure we had a path forward. Just as I hit send, my phone buzz with a text from Daniel.

"Made it home safe."

"Glad you're safe. Thanks again for everything today. Hope dinner wasn't too weird."

I laid back on the pillows like a teenager waiting to see if he would respond. He did.

"Wanna talk?"

It felt weird, like some sort of out-of-body experience. "Sure."

My phone rang almost instantly.

"Hello?"

"Hi," Daniel's voice resonated through the phone. "You, okay?"

"Yeah, I don't know. Is it weird that I want my mom to be happy, but I am worried about her dating?"

He chuckled quietly. "I think it is perfectly normal and sweet."

Sweet? He thinks I'm sweet. Why did this make me feel all tingly inside?

"I don't know what is wrong with me. My mother and I never bicker and I'm worried about this guy, Nick."

"I've known Nick for a few years. We hang out at each other's houses and have football parties with friends. He is a solid guy, not the sort of man to toy with your mom's affections. Definitely not a player."

"Probably, I…."

"Don't trust people easily."

I was stunned silent. He wasn't wrong. But how did he know?

"It just that....,"

"Harper, it's okay. It is a defense mechanism. Lots of people have them. I'm sorry to know that something happened to you in your past that made you have trust issues. But it isn't necessarily a bad thing until you allow it to be."

More silence at my end. What's happening here? I was having some sort of out-of-body experience where I spent the day with my nemesis, and he was giving me relationship advice like we were BFFs. I was freaking out. How did my world turn upside down so quickly?

"Thanks."

"It's getting late. I should let you get some sleep."

"Okay, I'll talk to you tomorrow."

"Talk to you soon."

"Bye."

The phone was silent. I gazed at the screen. He was gone. What the heck was going on?

Laying on my side, looking out the window as a snowflake landed. I raised my head up. Could it truly be snowing again? I drifted off to sleep in my childhood bed, watching the snow fall again.

∼

Nick

After I left Judy's, I was restless. I knew I wouldn't be able to sleep, so I went back to the store. One of my favorite places to unwind is my workshop, tucked in the back of Jansen's Hardware. The door groaned as I shut it behind me, sealing off the rest of the world. The scent of sawdust mingles with the sharp tang of paint, offering an inexplicable feeling of comfort and familiarity. It's quieter here, where the air is thick with the memories of old projects and the promise of new ones. There's a timeless quality to this space, where hours slip by unnoticed, each passing minute just a stroke in a much larger painting.

I ran my hand along the rough wood of my workbench, feeling the dents and scars carved into its surface over the years. Each groove tells a story—dents from hammers, scratches from hurried saws, splatters of paint from a forgotten project, remnants of glue that never quite came off. The shelves around me brim with half-finished toys: wooden trains with wheels waiting to be attached, dolls' houses needing a fresh coat of paint, and stuffed animals missing their last stitches. Each one represents a labor of love, a moment where I poured my energy and focus on creating something meaningful, hoping it brings joy to a little one spending the holiday in the hospital.

Usually, one or two of the staff from the hardware store join me after hours. They like the peace of the workshop as much as I do. But not tonight. The winter storm has kept staff and most of my customers away, but that's okay. I can use the quiet time. Christmas is mere weeks away, and I'm behind on the toys for the Children's Hospital. Santa's deadline waits for no one.

I pick up a sanding block and begin working on a rocking horse. The rhythmic sound of the block sliding across the wood was a steady companion to the ticking of the old wall clock. I sand the neck, smoothing its curves, but my mind drifts to thoughts of Judy Wade. Sweet Judy, with her flour-dusted apron and a laugh that sounds like crystal bells. I can picture her now, her hands kneading dough with the same care I use to shape these toys. The smell of freshly baked bread mingling with the soft hum of Christmas carols playing in her bakery.

Judy's a marvel, truly. At sixty-two, I never expected to feel like this again. It's not like me to get caught up in romance, but lately, just thinking about Judy sends my heart racing. I chuckle under my breath—a lovesick fool. What would the guys at the store say if they knew I'd been mooning over Judy like some teenager? And yet, here I am, a sixty-two-year-old man, my hands calloused from years of woodworking, feeling the flutter of young love all over again. It's strange, the way love can sneak up on you, like a spark catching kindling.

I've admired her from afar, stealing glances when she comes into the store for supplies. But it wasn't until recently that I started to imagine what it might be like to share more than polite nod or a brief conversation at the check-out desk. There's something special about her warmth, her serene smile. I can see her fitting into this world of mine, even though it's rough around the edges. I can picture her here, maybe helping me paint one of the toys, her fingers delicate and precise, her laughter filling the room.

I realize I've been sanding the same spot for far too long. The wood beneath my fingers is smooth as glass now.

"Get it together, Nick," I mutter to myself, shaking my head with a rueful grin.

I find it hard to focus when thoughts of Judy keep dancing through my mind like sugar plums on Christmas Eve. Setting down the sanding block, I take a step back and admire the rocking horse. It's shaping up nicely. The soft glow of the wood brings a sense of pride, a feeling I never tire of. Each toy is a piece of me, crafted with care, a small part of my heart carved and polished into something tangible. What Judy would say if she saw this? Would she think I'm a silly old man playing at being Santa in a dusty workshop? Or would she understand the magic that's in this space —the joy of creating something with your own two hands, of imagining a child's face lighting up when they unwrap one of these toys on Christmas morning?

Glancing at the clock—half-past midnight. It's late, and I still have a long list of toys to finish. There's something peaceful about working late into the night, when the world outside is quiet, and it's just me, my tools, and the promise of Christmas. I wonder if Judy feels the same satisfaction, I wonder, as she wipes down the counters, her eyes growing heavy with sleep.

The workshop feels a little colder as I hang up my apron. Without the soft hum of work, the silence settles in, wrapping around me like an old, familiar coat. The scent of sawdust lingers, a reminder of the unfinished toys waiting for my return tomorrow. But tonight, there's something else on my mind—a woman with flour on her hands and a laugh that makes my heart feel light.

It almost seems pointless to drive home for just a few hours. So, I settle into the small, worn-out sofa in the back office. I stretch out, but sleep evades me. My mind is buzzing with thoughts of Judy. I reach for my phone, staring at it, thumb hovering over her contact. Would it be presumptuous, I wonder, to send her a message? Maybe a text saying hello, something lighthearted, something that doesn't scream, "I'm thinking of you at one in the morning." I chuckle, shaking my head. What am I, a teenager? A message at this hour could easily come across as … well, odd. Besides, what would Judy think of me if she knew I was lying here, wide awake, contemplating sending her a midnight text?

Putting the phone down, I sigh. I've already risked coming off as intrusive once before, when I showed up at her bakery with her lost phone. She'd left it in the store, and I couldn't resist the excuse to bring it to her in person. I hadn't thought of the consequences, but now, in the quiet of the office, I cringe at the memory. She'd looked at me with those kind eyes, though, and maybe—just maybe—there'd been a flicker of something else there.

But tonight is different. Pacing the room, I try to shake off the nervous energy. I need to gain control over myself. Judy is the first woman in years who's made me feel this way, but she isn't the first. And the last thing I want is to make her uncomfortable. The room feels too small, too close, and I realize there's no sleeping tonight, not with these thoughts rattling around in my head like marbles in a tin can.

Finally, I sink back onto the sofa, resigning myself to a sleepless night. I'll go back to the workshop, I decide, maybe sand down one more piece, finish painting the train set. Anything to keep my hands busy and my mind from wandering. But even as I stand and reach for the door, I know it's no use. Because every piece of wood, every chisel, and brush in that workshop, seems to carry her memory, her laughter, her warmth. One day, I'll share this with her.

CHAPTER 8

Harper

December 3rd

I was dreaming of cinnamon buns and smores when I woke. Sitting up, I took in my surroundings; it wasn't a dream; I smelled cinnamon buns! My mom must be baking this morning.

I put on my slippers and rushed downstairs. My mom was icing buns on a tray just as I rushed in.

"Morning, mom."

"Morning sleepyhead. It's nearly nine."

"I knew I didn't have to go to work, so I didn't set an alarm. The wonderful scent of cinnamon buns woke me up."

"Come have a bun and coffee."

"How did I get so lucky to have the perfect mother?" I said, kissing her cheek on my way to the coffee.

"Just luck of the draw." She laughed. "Your brothers called to check on us."

"Oh, that was nice."

"I thought so."

I sat down at the table with a huge bun and a cup of black coffee. The sugar in the icing was sweet enough I wouldn't need anything more in the coffee.

"Okay mom, so tell me about Nick."

My mother turned and looked at me. "Honey, I don't want to start our day with an argument."

"I don't want to argue mom, I want you to be happy and I was probably a little overprotective yesterday. Can we start over?"

She pegged me with a stare and as if she might say no for a moment. But then she smiled. "Let me refill my coffee."

Taking a sip, I waited for her to settle into the chair across the table.

"Isn't he handsome?" She grinned.

"Yes, he is gorgeous. How old is he?"

"Do you mean, is he younger than me?" She raised her mug to her lips and waited.

"Yes, I suppose I do."

"Well, the answer is no. He is not older than me. We are the same age."

"He carries it well."

"What does that mean?" My mother seemed offended.

"I mean, I would have thought he was in his forties."

"And how old do I look?"

"You look thirty, mom, but the thing is, I know how old you are, so it doesn't count."

She thought about it for a minute. "Hmm, okay. Acceptable answer."

I laughed. "You have to understand, there is a snowstorm outside, parts of the city are without power, and a stranger shows up at your door with your long-lost cell phone? It sounds like a movie that doesn't end well."

She laughed out loud then. "You've seen too many of those movies."

"Perhaps."

"You're right. I don't know Nick intimately."

I wrinkled my nose at the thought. My mom continued, "I've seen him at the hardware store, although I will admit we've never talked until this week. But I've seen him helping other customers and talking to the staff. He has never acted rude to anyone and is a genuinely decent man." She paused and reached over and covered my hand with hers. "Good people still exist in this world."

I had some doubts on that subject, but instead of voicing them, I said, "So, tell me more." I said, then taking a bite from the cinnamon bun.

"Apart from being gorgeous, he played football in college. Served in the military. He has a degree in engineering. He worked in the construction field for several years, retired and bought the hardware store."

I nodded for her to continue.

"Nick spends his free time watching football with his friends. He loves hiking, sailing, surfing, pretty much anything that keeps him outside and in shape."

I nodded, popping more cinnamon bun in my mouth because what had started out as a way to keep my comments to myself had turned into a full-on addiction to the icing and I couldn't stop eating it. So far, I had to admit that Nick sounded like a stable guy and not some snowstorm serial killer.

"I'm happy for you if you're happy, mom."

"Well, it isn't anything serious. We are just friends, but I am happy, and I wouldn't mind if it turned into something more."

I sat back, looking at my mother in a different light. She was my mom, my savior, my best friend, but now I viewed her as an equal, recognizing that she had also experienced past pain and avoided relationships. I was genuinely happy she was doing something for herself. I hoped she didn't get hurt.

"So, tell me about Daniel," she said, giving me that look that said she already knew the answer.

"Not much to tell. He was nice enough to let me hang out at his place yesterday while I got a little work done."

"And you brought him to dinner?"

"If I hadn't, I wouldn't have been able to come see you, so I had little choice."

"Hmm," using a tone that made me think she didn't believe me.

"Which reminds me, I need to check and see if my apartment has power yet." I whipped out my phone as a distraction to wherever my mother was taking this conversation and logged into the resident's portal. "Yes!"

"The power is back on?"

"Yes, that means I can go home and start tossing food out of my freezer."

"Oh no, why didn't you say something? We could have packed it up and brought it over here."

"I didn't think about it. It's okay. I hadn't been to the grocery store in a few days. The loss isn't that big of a deal." I sighed. "I should have put it all in a cooler and put it on the balcony."

"That's a clever thought."

"The question is, how do I get home?"

"I'll take you."

"Mom, I don't want you driving in this."

"Don't be silly, besides I need to check on the bakery."

"I hope you didn't lose power."

"We have backup generators for the refrigeration and the worst I'd have to do is reboot the computers."

I nodded. My mom was a smart woman, and she would have systems in place to prevent loss of inventory. I needed to think like her more.

"Let's have another cup of coffee and then I will drive you home."

"I'll go with you to the bakery in case you need any help."

"Deal."

We made it across town safely. Snow still covered the residential streets, but the main roads were cleared, although icy patches remained. When we got to my apartment, I noticed management had put up fliers informing us they had placed large trash containers with lids in the alley out back for our use for spoiled food.

I opened the freezer and started removing the frozen prepared meals and ice cream.

"You weren't kidding, Harper; you need to eat better."

"I only eat these in a pinch. In the fridge should be some wilted veggies." I stood aside and opened the fridge. The stench of warm, spoiled milk and yogurt greeted us.

"Whoa! I'll grab another trash bag," My mom covered her nose and reached for the roll of bags on the counter. "Where's your phone? You need to document all of this for insurance purposes."

"Claim one hundred dollars' worth of food so they can jack my rates up? No, thank you. I'll take the hit."

My mom laughed, "Practical."

"Gotta look at the big picture. "A hundred dollars now isn't worth hundreds per year down the road."

"True. Do you have a hundred dollars to throw away?"

"Never, but one is better than two or three."

"Okay, okay. You do what you think is best."

I could tell she didn't agree with me, but I'd rather file a claim for something more than a hundred dollars. It's like if my neighbor upstairs has a water leak and floods my entire apartment or something. After lugging two trash bags of food down to the dumpsters, we went back to my apartment.

"Why don't you pack some things and come stay with me until you can the stores reopen, and you can restock?"

"Thanks, mom. I can have groceries delivered."

"And how long will that take? The stores that can even deliver are going to be swamped. Let's check and make sure things are secure here and pack a bag. You can work remotely from my house as easily as you can from here."

She had a point, and it might be lovely to spend some time with my mom. "Okay."

Mom smiled and clapped her hands. "Wonderful."

With my refrigerator cleaned, we headed to the bakery.

"It seems we never lost power." Mom announced, unlocking the door and checking the refrigerators. I'm going to walk down the street and if any of the other businesses are open yet.

"Okay, I'll stay and keep an eye on the place."

"Thanks."

Mom reported back that other business owners near the bakery were checking on their stores, and everyone was trying to reopen as soon as possible. Mom and I spent the rest of the afternoon doing what we needed to do to get the bakery ready to open the next day. I called staff to see who could come in while mom prepped dough and other ingredients.

We found a grocery store open and restocked my fridge before going back to my apartment for the night. It made sense for mom to stay with me to be closer to the bakery until the roads were in better condition.

After dinner, we sat together, watching the weather and hoping the temperatures would finally rise above freezing, allowing the snow to melt, and life to return to normal. But fate had other plans. The forecast predicted freezing temperatures for the rest of the week, and the risk of pipes bursting became a real possibility.

"Mom, what should we do?"

"I don't know. There isn't much you can do about the pipes in your apartment. Let's hope they are already insulated."

"What about the bakery? I hope everything is okay."

"Not much I can do about it tonight." Mom frowned. "I was going to try to open in the morning at least have a little something for the folks in the immediate area."

"At least Jazz can come in; she lives close enough to walk if necessary. The others I told them not to worry about it, come if they could, but no worries if they couldn't."

Mom nodded. "Me, you and Jazz can offer a limited menu, anyway."

"I'll do whatever I can to help."

"You are so sweet. Thank you. We better go to sleep if we are going to open tomorrow."

"You're right." My mother would need to get up at four in the morning to go to the bakery and have fresh croissants, bagels, and donuts for the morning rush. I wasn't looking forward to that part.

The next morning, the alarm went off way too early, but I got up, showered, and dressed. My mom was already awake and making coffee before her turn in the bathroom.

We walked the short distance to the bakery. Despite wearing multiple layers with an outer shell, the frigid wind still managed to cut through it all.

My mom unlocked the door. "If you'll start the coffee, I'll start on everything else."

"Absolutely."

I wasn't sure how I was going to make the coffee with my

hands frozen inside my mittens that I wore over my gloves. I peeled everything off and rubbed my hands together. Then went to work on the large commercial grade coffee makers. The bakery had two, and I was sure we would need both today.

With the coffee started, I rummaged in the storage room and found a chalkboard sign and wrote open, hot coffee on it and stuck it in the snow out front.

I found a couple of balloons and taped them to the sign; with the hope they would stay in inflated in these wintery temperatures.

My mom was already working on pastry dough.

"What else can I do to help?"

"Could you boot up the computers for the day?"

I was logging my mom's username and password into the computer when Jazz came in.

"Good morning!" She called out in true morning person fashion.

"Hi, Jazz."

"Hi Harper, helping out today?"

"As much as I can, mom's already at it in the back."

"Got it."

Jasmine, or Jazz, as we called her, was my mom's most senior employee. She was entrusted with the recipe for the flakiest croissant recipe. Even I didn't know that one, not that it would have made much difference. I didn't have the patience for all that rolling, chilling, rolling business.

The coffee finished brewing, and I poured three mugs and carried them to the kitchen.

"Mom, Jazz, coffee's ready."

"Oh, thank you, sweetie."

Jazz came over and took hers, quickly taking a sip.

"Oh, that is liquid gold." She sighed and went back to work.

"I'll keep an eye out for customers unless you need help back here."

"You could be our runner." Mom suggested.

"Can do!"

I spent an hour running around grabbing things they needed for whichever pastry they were working on. Mom was keeping it simple in case there weren't many customers.

Soon, the front case was filled with croissants and bagels. Then mom made up some eggs, and we had egg and cheese bagels while sitting around talking about our predictions for the weather.

My phone buzzed with a text from Christina. "Where are you today?"

"At the bakery helping mom."

"On my way!"

It didn't take long before Christina arrived.

"Good morning, everyone!" Christina called as she came through the front door.

"Morning!" I greeted, happy to see a friendly face. "How much did your mom have to pay you to get up this early?" She laughed.

"The promise of cinnamon buns."

"Oooh, that would for me, too." She giggled.

The door opened again. Our latest customer turned out to be two shop owners from down the street. Soon, the place filled up and everyone started talking about the weather. The café was becoming packed. Christina was immediately pressed into service. One customer asked me about the tree lighting ceremony.

"What's the point of a tree lighting without a crowd? Kinda kills the mood." I responded.

"Why not live stream it on social media?" The customer suggested.

"That is a fantastic idea! Thank you!"

Excusing myself, I dashed to the office to grab my laptop from my bag, emailing the communications department and my boss.

I only had to wait a few minutes before I received a reply from my boss. "Fantastic idea. Make it happen."

"Yes!" I pumped my fist in the air.

An hour and a half later, we had a plan. Emails would go out to newsletter subscribers and the webpage would be updated. The TV and radio stations would receive press releases: anyone who could safely attend the tree lighting on Thursday was welcome, and for those who couldn't, we'd live stream it. I hurried back to the front of the bakery and announced the plan to the patrons. A round of applause followed.

My mom smiled. "Guess I'll be open late that day."

"You'll sell a lot of hot chocolate." I laughed.

Christina glanced around; "we need to decorate this place. It needs to be more festive."

"I've got a few decorations in the back, but most of them are at home," Mom offered.

"Let's put them up and if we need more, I have some at home."

My mom smiled. "That's a plan."

It felt like a weight lift off my shoulders. I emailed the committee members, including Daniel, to inform them of the new plan. Everyone was eager, and suddenly, the snow felt a little less depressing. Sipping a cup of coffee, I sat at a table, savoring the comforting aroma of warm baked goods. After months of effort, I was finally accomplishing something, and it felt good. I was in my happy place.

CHAPTER 9

Judy

The Christmas season was my favorite time of year, and the fact that we had snow for the tree lighting ceremony felt perfect to me. I hoped plenty of people would come out to watch in person, rather than just watch from home on the internet. There's something magical about standing in the cold, hands wrapped around a warm cup of cocoa or coffee. Braving the cold made the event feel more festive, more real.

I hadn't heard from Nick since dinner at my house, and I hoped he wasn't dealing with a power outage or frozen pipes. Taking a deep breath, I reminded myself not to jump in too fast. Should I text him? I stared at my phone, then decided against it and slipped it back into my pocket.

I couldn't blame Harper for her initial reaction to Nick. To be fair, her father hadn't been a shining example of a healthy relationship. He made our lives hell when he was around, yet when he left, it broke Harper's heart. She never had many boyfriends as a teenager, and none of them were serious. I wasn't the best example either—I kept my own relationships hidden from the kids or avoided them altogether.

I realized Harper had feelings for Daniel, even though she kept pushing them away. Daniel's affection for her was undeniable, but he appeared to be taking his time. I wanted to tell him to push a little harder—if he waited for Harper to make the first move, he'd be waiting a long time.

"Judy?" Jazz's voice brought be out of my head space.

"Yes?"

"We are getting low on scones. Should I make some more?"

I checked the time; we had a steady stream of customers so we could sell some more.

"Yes, go ahead."

Jazz smiled and went to work. She loved baking as much as I did. Whatever we didn't sell, I would take to the shelter. I'm sure they would appreciate it, especially today. I hoped everyone who needed a warm place had made their way to one of the shelters or churches who opened their doors during the winter months.

Jazz was working in the kitchen; Harper was on her laptop at a corner table. Taking a moment for myself, the aroma of coffee and baked goods had a way of soothing my soul. I stared at the window for the moment, watching people ice skating. Ice skating?

"Harper, are any of the city offices or services open today?"

"No, mom."

"There are people ice skating, and I don't think anyone is manning the skate rental booth."

Harper rushed over to stand next to me. We peered out the window for a few minutes.

She smiled. "It appears people who have their own skates are taking advantage of the rink."

I smiled back at her. "Great. That means people will come to the tree lighting ceremony if they are in the area."

Harper's smile widened. "This might work out after all." She ran and grabbed her coat.

"Where are you going?"

"Mom, I'm going to go talk to them and ask if they would come back out for the tree lighting."

"Okay, be careful." I shook my head as she dashed down the sidewalk.

My gaze shifted from Harper rushing to greet the ice skaters to a mom and little boy, who looked as if they were nearly frozen. "Hello, come in and warm up."

The woman smiled. "Thank you. We were making snow angels and now we are positively glacial." She said while helping her son take off his coat and hat.

I kneeled down. "How about some hot cocoa?"

The little boy nodded shyly.

"You got it." I stood up and asked the mom. "What would you like?"

"Hot tea?"

"Coming up. Do you want a scone, croissant, or anything?"

"Cookie!" the little boy said hopefully.

The mom rolled her eyes. He'll be restless the rest of the day. She looked past me. "Do you have cookies?"

"Normally, we do, but I didn't make anything today. I wasn't sure if we would have any customers."

"Mommy!" the boy cried.

I could tell the mom was exhausted. "Have you guys been in the house for a while?"

"Yeah, he's been staying indoors a lot the past couple of days."

"I have an idea. Why don't you have a bagel sandwich with your tea? And if you don't mind, he can help me make cookies."

She thought about it for a minute.

"You can come sit in the back with us if you like, or you can take a break and have a moment out here."

She smiled, "You're a lifesaver."

"I raised three children. I know that look."

"Thanks! Cooper, do you want to make cookies?"

He gazed up at his mom and then at me. "My name is Judy; we can go in the back and make any kind of cookie you like."

A huge smiled covered his face. "Choco Cookie!"

I laughed, "Sure," I turned to his mom to confirm that he meant.

"Chocolate chip."

An hour later, I was sending Cooper and his mom home refreshed and with a bag of freshly baked cookies.

I was standing at the door waving goodbye to them when a familiar voice spoke low behind me. It sent a shiver down my spine.

He took a deep breath. "Hmm, warm cookies. Is it you or the store?"

I spun around, feeling the heat rise in my cheeks. Nick was grinning at me.

"What are you doing here?"

"I desperately needed a muffin."

I wasn't sure if my face could get any hotter, but it did. "Well, I'm sure we can accommodate you."

"Hmm," He grinned at my embarrassment. Something about Nick made me blush with every word he spoke. It was exasperating.

Jazz her raised her eyebrows in my direction before turning away.

"Have a seat and I'll pour you some coffee." I used the coffee as an excuse to put some distance between us and try to control the blushing.

Nick chose a seat in the corner.

I walked over to his table with a fresh cup of coffee. "What would you like? We have fresh from the oven cookies, also croissants that I can use to make a sandwich, bagels, and an assortment of muffins."

"I'd like a blueberry muffin and a chocolate chip cookie." Nick gave me the most charming, lopsided grin.

"I'll be right back."

"Judy, are you okay?" Jazz brought me back to the task at hand.

"I'm fine, thanks."

"Can I help you?"

"No, I've got it." I rushed to put the coffee back and then warm a muffin for Nick. "Oh Jazz, you could grab me some butter to go with this muffin."

"You got it."

I took a deep breath, trying to steady my nerves. As I plated a muffin and a cookie. Jazz was back with the butter, and I placed that on the plate as well.

"Here we go," I said, putting the plate in front of Nick.

He gave me a warm smile. "Thank you. Can you join me?"

Despite my desire, I couldn't bring myself to do it. I looked back at the kitchen. "Sorry, I wish I could. The kitchen needs cleaning. Four-year-olds make the biggest mess."

"You start your employees young, don't you?" He gave me a quizzical look.

"What? Oh no, I had a young mother and little boy in earlier. The little boy helped me in the kitchen while his mom had some much-needed alone time." I laughed nervously.

He reached out and lightly squeezed my hand. "You're a sweet woman, Judy Wade. I wouldn't dream of keeping you from your work."

My cheeks were reddening again. "I'll be back in a few minutes." I rushed to the back. Why was my heart pounding in my chest so hard?

Jazz came over to the workspace where I was standing. "What are you doing?"

"Cleaning."

"Yes, I see that. But why are you avoiding that gorgeous man? Go sit with him and I'll clean."

I stopped and stared at her. "Since when are you the matchmaker?"

"Go."

I wanted to hug her. Hesitating at the door, Jazz shoved me out.

I walked back to where Nick sat alone. "Hey," I said, not sure what else to say.

Nick looked up, surprised, and smiled. "Hey, I'm glad you could join me."

"Yeah, me too," I sat down, wiping the flour off my hands and onto my apron. "How's the store? Did it survive the storm?"

"Oh yeah, it's a solid building. No problems."

"Good." I don't know why I felt so nervous. I had spent all night talking to Nick and felt like I knew him for years. But the butterflies in my stomach were making me uncomfortable.

"I'm glad it looks like the bakery survived." He glanced around.

"Yes, we were lucky. I thought I would open today and offer at least a few items. I wasn't sure if there would be any customers but, it has been a steady stream all morning."

"That's awesome."

He sipped his coffee. I stood up. "Do you need more coffee?"

Nick reached out and gently took my hand. "Judy, I need you to be still for a moment."

I sank back down into the chair.

"Is everything alright?"

Looking up at him, hoping I hadn't given him the wrong impression and that he didn't think I was avoiding him. "Everything is wonderful." I smiled back at him.

"Then why don't you take a deep breath and relax for a minute?"

Closing my eyes, I took a deep breath. I immediately felt calmer.

A customer came in, but Jazz's immediate help made me feel like I wasn't needed at the moment.

"Why don't you have some coffee with me?" Nick asked.

"I'm feeling the effects of too much caffeine."

He nodded. "That would explain it, then."

"Explain what?"

"Why you seem jittery." He gave me a devious grin. "And here I thought it was me."

Tongue tied for a minute; I finally spit out some words. "I enjoy spending time with you." Then I nearly bit my tongue for betraying my feelings. Nick cocked an eyebrow at me and took my hand.

"I love spending time with you and I'm hoping I can do more of that, if you will allow me."

"Well, uh yes. I mean," My brain had officially shut down. I couldn't string together words in the correct order to form a coherent sentence.

Nick saved me from myself. "Mario's is open. How about I come back by here after work and take you to dinner?".

"Yes, that will be lovely."

He nodded and reached for his wallet. I threw up my hands. "No, it's on the house."

"Judy, I can't…."

"Yes, you can, and you will." I said firmly.

He conceded defeat. "Thank you. Five-thirty?"

"Perfect."

Nick nodded and stood to leave. He let his gaze linger for a long moment and then strode out the door. Watching him as he pulled on his coat and hat while moving down the sidewalk, I could hear the faint sound of giggling and saw Harper, Christina, and Jazz hiding behind the counter like schoolgirls.

"What are you two doing?"

"Nothing, cleaning,"

"Hmmm, hmm." I walked behind the counter to check on the progress in the kitchen, but Harper and Jazz were right. They had been cleaning. I had nothing left to do.

"Good job, ladies."

The door opened and a crew of city employees came in from the cold. It took all of us to serve everyone. The rest of the day was a blur as more and more people found we were open. I called the other employees to asking how many could make it to work the next day. If today was any indication, tomorrow was going to be busy.

CHAPTER 10

※

Nick

There was no time to run home and change before picking Judy up for dinner. I kept a few essentials tucked away in my desk drawer, so I freshened up—combed my hair, shaved, and splashed on a bit of aftershave.

Feeling somewhat presentable, I headed over to the bakery. I parked around back beside Judy's car, then strolled to the front door. The sign read "Closed," but I gave the door a try anyway, and it opened. I stepped inside, the familiar warmth of the place wrapping around me. "Hello?" I called out, my voice soft in the quiet space.

Judy stepped out from the kitchen area. "Hi, come on in. I'll get my purse."

I waited. Judy reappeared, and I was pretty sure she hadn't been wearing that black sweater earlier in the day. She was wearing black jeans, snow boots and a black sweater with gold threads woven throughout, causing it to shimmer in the light. The way it complimented the blond streaks in her light brown hair took my breath away.

"My truck is out back if you want to drive instead of walk."

"Oh, okay, do you mind driving?"

"Not at all." I smiled, stepping aside to allow her to lock the door, then followed her behind the counter and through the kitchen. Everything was spotless and ready for the next day.

Stepping out the back door into the frosty air, I placed my hand on her back delicately to ensure she didn't fall on her way to the truck. She smiled as I helped her up and then I rushed to the driver's side to climb in next to her.

I made my way through the streets to the far side of City Center. Most of the roads were clear, with only a few lingering patches of ice hiding in the shadows of the trees.

Arriving at Mario's Italian Restaurant; I found a parking spot on the street. Inside, the restaurant was warm and bathed in soft light and a little crowded.

"Wow, I hope we can get a table." Judy said, looking around.

"No worries, I had called ahead."

Judy raised an eyebrow at me. "Mario doesn't take reservations."

I grinned, "That is true in the traditional sense, but let's just say I did him a favor in the recent past."

Anna Maria greeted us, "Nick, so good to see you. Judy, how is the bakery?"

"Good, just reopened today."

"Ah, wonderful. Right this way. I have a table for you."

She seated us at a cozy table by an electric fireplace and a delightful view of the snow outside.

A waiter materialized with a small candle in a red jar.

"What would you like to drink, wine perhaps?"

"Yes, an apéritif would be nice." I answered. The waiter nodded and left.

Judy glanced around and then at me. "This is lovely."

I didn't need to look around the room. Everything I wanted to see was sitting in front of me. "Yes, it is."

Judy blushed a little.

"I'm sorry if I make you feel uncomfortable."

"No, no," she protested.

The waiter returned with the wine, cutting her words short. Judy recovered, and the waiter poured the wine.

I held up my glass. "To storms that bring new friends together."

She smiled and returned my toast.

"Hmm, that is delicious. You have good taste, Mr. Tanner."

Words failed me. It had been easy to talk to her sitting at her kitchen table a few nights ago, but now, in a more date-like setting, I found it hard to know what to talk about.

Judy finally broke the ice. "How was business today?"

"It was pretty good, a little slower than before the storm."

"Oh, I'm sorry."

"No, it's okay. It will pick up again. No worries. It is better if people stay off the roads right now, anyway."

Glancing out the window, she replied. "It's surprising it hasn't melted yet."

"I'm afraid we might be in for another round."

"No," she gasped, leaning forward. "Don't say that. Harper will lose her mind."

I chuckled.

Judy rolled her eyes. "Thank goodness she found out they can do the lighting this weekend and offer it virtually as well. Harper has refocused her efforts to organize that."

"She works as hard as you do." I took another sip of the wine, feeling a little more relaxed.

The waiter came back with bread and took our order. "Oh, and Ms. Anna says to save room for dessert."

Judy and I gazed at each other. "I wonder what she had planned?"

Judy smiled, "No telling. But I wouldn't mind if it was a cannoli."

"Me either."

The conversation came easier now, and we were discussing our bucket lists of places we'd like to visit when the food arrived.

"I'd like to go to Europe and visit as many countries at Christmas as possible." Judy was saying.

"That sounds like fun. You could buy a rail pass."

"Oh, that would be perfect!"

We made hypothetical plans for a European Christmas vacation. I loved the way her eyes lit up while we talked. Her excitement over the possibilities of what each country might be like.

Dessert turned out to be a tiramisu cheesecake.

"Oh my gosh, this looks decadent." Judy exclaimed.

Anna came over to check on us, and she and Judy discussed the particulars of making such a decadent dessert. I couldn't comprehend any of it.

When the meal was over, I didn't want the evening to end. We strolled back to my truck. Judy turned her eyes up to the night sky. It was too cloudy for stars. She closed her eyes and took a deep breath. "Isn't that wonderful?"

"What's that?"

"The clean night air."

Taking my own deep breath. "Yes, it is. Is it too cold for a walk?"

She gave me a warm smile. "Not at all."

Offering her my arm to help steady us both, and we took

a leisurely stroll down the sidewalk. "I can't wait for all the Christmas lights to be turned on."

"Have you ever been to the light display at the botanical gardens?" I asked, an idea blooming in my mind.

"No, I haven't."

"Wanna go with me? I think you would love it."

"When?"

"This weekend, Harper's tree lighting is Saturday, right?"

"Yes,"

"How about we go to the botanical gardens on Sunday and have dinner over in Norfolk?"

She squeezed my arm, "it sounds perfect."

I felt her shiver a little. "Ready to go back?"

"I am a little cold."

"Say no more." I turned us back towards the truck. "You feel okay to drive home?" We had little to drink at dinner and the frosty night air certainly got rid of all the cobwebs we may have had from a heavy meal and wine. But I wanted to make sure she was okay.

"I'm fine, thank you. Actually, I'm staying at Harper's. It's just a few blocks from the bakery."

She directed me to Harper's apartment. I pulled up to the curb, and we sat for a moment; I got the impression she wasn't quite ready for the evening to end either, but I wasn't sure what to do or say next. Inviting her back to my house seemed cliche`.

"Do you want me to walk you to the door?"

"I'll be okay, but thank you."

I nodded. "Do you have your cell phone?"

She laughed, "Yes, right here."

I smiled. "Can I call you later or will that be too awkward with Harper around?"

"I'd like that. I would like to know you made it home safely." She smiled.

"I had a wonderful evening, Judy."

"Me, too."

"Here, let me open the door for you."

I had an overwhelming urge to kiss her and at our age, the cat-and-mouse game of dating felt unnecessary. So, I leaned in, giving her the chance to pull away if she wanted to. She didn't. Instead, she leaned closer.

I touched her lips lightly, fighting the urge to embrace her with a deeper kiss. When we each took a small step back, she smiled up at me. "I enjoy spending time with you, Nick."

"Me too. It's like we... share a similar history." Those weren't the right words, but I couldn't think of a better way to describe what I was feeling. It was like she'd always been a part of me, even though we'd only met a week ago.

"Soul mates," she whispered.

She was right, of course, as if she could read my mind. "Soul mates," I repeated.

Reaching up, Judy gently grabbed my coat, pulling me down to her for another kiss. I wrapped my arms around her to hold her as close as I possibly could. We stood for several minutes until her car compressor made a noise and brought us back to reality.

"I should probably go; I've got to get up early to be back here by five." She said reluctantly.

"That early?"

"Yeah, I'm going to have to do a lot more baking tomorrow than I did today."

"Okay. I'll call you tomorrow." We were still locked in our embrace. I slowly released her. "

"You need to get back in your truck where it's warm." She scolded.

"Yes, ma'am." I couldn't argue with her. The absence of her body left me cold and shivering.

I watched her walk into the apartment building. I sat in

my truck thinking about her kiss and her declaration that we were soul mates. It had been a long time since I'd dated anyone, and I wasn't sure I'd ever felt this way before. I'd never been married—much to my mother's disappointment. Just never found the right woman, and I was always too busy with the military, then college, and finally running the hardware store.

My mother passed last year, so she would never get to meet Judy, which I deeply regret. Mom would've loved her. It's funny how life works out. They say you get what you need when you need it, and I can't argue with that right now. Before I met Judy, my life felt lonely. I had friends, but most of them had wives or girlfriends, and I often wondered what I had besides work. Now, I had my answer—Judy.

CHAPTER 11

Harper

After walking home from the bakery, it felt good to be back in my own space. I didn't waste any time turning up the thermostat and making a cup of tea. I had work to do to get this ready for this weekend, starting with sending out a flurry of emails to staff and volunteers to see who was available to kick things off.

I took a break to grab another cup of tea and settle back under a warm blanket. A message popped up on the city's internal chat program from Daniel.

"You're working late again."

"So are you, apparently. My mom is out to dinner with Nick, so I thought I'd get a little work done." I smiled to myself. "What's your excuse for working at this hour?"

"Budget reports still have to be done, and I can do those from anywhere. Do you need help with the tree lighting? What can I do?"

I sat, starting at the screen. Even though Daniel had been kind and helped me when I was stranded without heat, I still wasn't sure how I felt about him. He seemed nice enough, but I had spent so much time building a wall between us over budget issues, I was finding it difficult to let that go.

"I've reached out to the staff and volunteers, so until I hear from them, I don't know where I need help yet. But I appreciate the offer."

"The offer stands. Call on me anytime."

How could he be this nice? Didn't he realize he was destroying my meticulously crafted opinions of him? I couldn't bring myself to admit I was entirely mistaken. "Thank you. I will warn you now. I might have to take up on that offer."

"Like I said, anytime."

I clicked like on his comment and went back to work on my emails.

After an hour my stomach reminded me, I hadn't eaten since this morning. I gave up on working and closed the laptop. Padding into the kitchen, I tried to decide what I felt like making for dinner. My phone rang. Sighing, I reached into my pocket, annoyed that I would not accomplish anything today.

"Hello."

"Hey. Wow, you sound grumpy." Christina groused.

"Sorry, I didn't look at the screen and I'm just hungry."

"Then it is a good thing I am on my way with pizza. Do you have beer, or should I stop?"

Checking the fridge, "I have beer."

"I'll be there in five."

And she was gone. I wish I could solve all my problems so easily. Pulling plates from the cabinet, I then went to turn on the TV and cue up a streaming channel. Christina let herself in with her keycard I had given her to the building and my apartment. I had one for hers as well.

"Hey, I'm here!"

"Hi!" I greeted her and grabbed the bag she was carrying while she took the pizza to the dining table. "Dinner and a movie?"

"I have the TV up and the beer is cold."

"Good, because I am starving." Christina tossed her backpack into the corner and opened up the bag to produce garlic knots.

I inhaled the aroma. "This is why you are my best friend."

She laughed. "I know."

I grabbed the beers while she filled our plates with pizza and knots.

"What are we watching tonight?" I asked, settling in with my dinner.

"The grinch and frosty are coming on tonight."

"Awesome," I grabbed the remote to change us over to Primetime TV to watch our favorite childhood Christmas shows.

Once settled under our blankets with pizza and beer, I was feeling much better.

"How's work going?" Christina asked between bites.

"The tree lighting will be this weekend. And as part of that, we will also do a live stream event for those who can't come. The crews have cleared the streets and parking lots. So, I think it will be safe for those who want to come."

"That's awesome!"

"Yeah, I don't know why I never thought of doing a virtual event before. It makes so much sense."

"Because you are too busy trying to solve all the problems at once."

"Hush! The commercial is over." I felt Christina's eyes on me, but she hushed, and the show started.

We sat enjoying our sofa picnic and singing along with the songs.

"What about you? Is the library reopening soon?"

We are following everyone else's schedule, so maybe on Monday. In the meantime, we were doing virtual story times this week. "Can you imagine being stuck in the house with kids under the age of ten? I'd go crazy and so would they."

"Yeah, it's hard because everyone wants to play in the snow, but then you're cold and wet, and you have to go back inside."

Christina laughed, "Are we still talking about the little ones, or you?"

"Hilarious."

"Have you talked to Daniel anymore?"

I gave her my best exacerbated look. "Why do you ask?"

"So that would be a yes." Christina giggled.

"I have to talk to him about work."

"Was it about work?"

"Yes,"

"When?"

"Earlier this evening, before you called."

Christina stopped what she was doing. "What did you talk about?"

"Work." I dried the plates and put them away.

"You're impossible."

"Why?"

"That is a question for the universe and your mother."

"Ha Ha, you're so funny."

"Why can't you see he's into you?"

"Why do I care?"

He is good looking. He is smart. He is charming. He is into you.

"Like that's a reason."

"Oh well excuse me, I didn't realize you had so many men knocking down your door."

"That isn't what I meant, and you know it."

"Hey if you don't want to date, that is your prerogative. But I wouldn't be so quick to turn him away. In fact, if you're not into him, maybe you could set me up."

"Will not!"

"I knew it. You do like him!"

"No, I mean yes. I mean, he isn't that bad, but if I didn't like him, why would I set the two of you up and then have to work with him all the time?"

"It was just a thought; you could spread the wealth and send me your discarded suitors."

I was feeling frustrated. "I don't have any suitors."

"Why don't you like Daniel, seriously?"

"Because he is a scrooge and a miser. He doesn't support the tree lighting. I wonder if he even likes Christmas."

"You are completely mental." She snagged another beer from the fridge.

"Why would you say that?"

After inviting you into his home when you were literally left in the cold, he spent the day watching Christmas movies with you.

Christina had a wonderful way of reminding me how ridiculous I could be. Which was incredibly annoying. She had a point, and I didn't like that part of myself, but I struggled to control it.

"What did he say when you talked to him tonight?"

"While I was online working, he sent me a message asking if I need help with the tree lighting." I said sheepishly.

"Hmm, sounds like someone who likes Christmas and you. Maybe someone who wishes he could help finance the event more, but his hands are tied by rules and regulations. I mean, you're not the only department asking for more money. Do you have any idea how many programs we want to do and can't because there isn't enough money in the budget for it?"

I blinked.

"Let me give you a different perspective. What if Daniel thought the way you did?"

"What do you mean?"

"What if he goes over to his friend's house to watch football and he tells his friend about this woman at work, who is always asking for money for a program they can't support financially no matter how good of an idea it is and then she gives him the cold shoulder because he said he didn't have the money? And his perception of you is that you only care about yourself and your projects and none of the other city goals or activities."

I sank down into a chair. "I'm a horrible person."

"No, you're not, sweetie, but you get too focused sometimes and you can't see the forest for the trees."

"Nope, I'm one hundred percent a horrible person."

Christina sighed, "Okay let's say for argument's sake you're a horrible person. What are you going to do about it?"

"I know what I want to do, but I don't know how to do it."

"And what is that?"

"Stop being so judgmental."

Christina laughed, "I think you are being too harsh on yourself. Try to relax a little. You are so focused because you want to do a good job, and you worry about things going wrong." She put her arms around me. "It's okay if things go wrong sometimes."

"Uh, I don't know about that."

"You need to change your perspective about things, like you thought Daniel was a scrooge, but he was happy to spend the day with you and offered to help you with the tree lighting."

"So true."

"You should text him back and ask him to help you."

"I think I will. What should I ask him to do?"

"That part doesn't matter." She laughed.

"Oh." I wasn't so sure, but I was willing to let it go for now.

"So, what is next?" Christina asked.

"What did you have in mind?"

"I thought we could binge the Hallmark channel."

"Sounds good to me."

Mom came in just as we were about to start a movie.

"Hi mom, how was dinner with Nick?"

"Yeah, Judy, come tell us everything!" Christina chimed in.

"Okay," I said, kicking off her shoes. "But only on the condition you share your beer."

"Deal!" we said in unison.

We sat up like a bunch of teenagers, listening to the details of my mom's date. I had to admit I was envious that she had a better social life than I did. But was genuinely happy for her.

I woke the next morning, stretched out on the sofa and Christina in the kitchen, making coffee.

"What time is it?"

"Nearly seven."

"Why are you up so early?"

Christina walked in carrying a cup of coffee. "You'd be up this early if you had to go into the office."

"Maybe, but the point is, I don't have to go into the office."

"For a perfectionist, you sure are grumpy in the morning."

"You knew that already." I breathed in the steam from the coffee before taking a sip.

"I can't believe I slept on the sofa all night."

"Me, too. Your mom took the bedroom."

"Mom! Oh my gosh, what time is it? I told her I would help her at the bakery."

"Here, she left you this note next to the coffeemaker."

Morning, baby cakes.

I wanted to let you sleep; you need the rest. You can come to the bakery, and I'll make breakfast.

Love,

Mom

P.S. Bring Christina

After drinking more coffee, I was feeling fractionally more human. "Ah, this is good."

"I've got to log into work, do you mind?" Christina said, pulling out her laptop.

"Go ahead. I'm going to have a little more coffee and then check my email."

I sat back and thought about what Christina had said last night. Maybe my focus was excessive, turning into hyperfocus. If I was honest, I wasn't enjoying the holiday season and why was that? Because I was looking at things all wrong. Instead of enjoying the rare snow days, I was only concerned with how it messed up my schedule.

Picking up my phone. I was pretty sure I had Daniel's personal cell phone number. "Hey this is Harper. If you're not busy today, I thought maybe we could meet for lunch?"

It was a bold move, but I didn't care. I needed to act like a normal human for once. It was a few minutes before I got a response.

"Hey, out jogging. Lunch sounds fantastic. I'll text you when I'm back in my car."

"Sounds good."

I opened my laptop and pulled up my emails. It was going to be a busy day.

CHAPTER 12

❄

*H*arper

After a quick run through of my emails, Christina and I headed to the bakery until lunchtime. I felt only slightly guilty for ditching home and Christina for Daniel. We agreed to meet at Midtown Eats, a place we could both walk to. I didn't mind getting out of my apartment for a bit, plus it gave me a chance to walk by the Christmas tree site and check on the progress. We had three days until showtime.

Since I couldn't control the weather or its aftermath, there was only so much I could do to ensure everything went smoothly. Christina was right—I worried too much. But letting go was always easier said than done.

I spotted Daniel walking up the sidewalk, looking like he'd just stepped off the cover of a winter sport outfitter magazine. He wore jeans, duck boots, and a heavy brown jacket with a fleece collar, topped off with a knit hat. His dark hair peeked out from under the hat, giving him a rugged, handsome look. I paused, admiring the view, when he glanced up and caught me staring. Embarrassed, I waved and blushed. He smiled as he approached, his smile only enhancing his good looks. "Right on time," he said.

I wasn't sure if he meant me or himself. "Perfect timing."

Daniel reached for the door. "Shall we?"

I nodded and stepped in ahead of him.

The place was packed; people filled every nook and cranny. Tables lined the walls, with bench seats and chairs along the aisle. Daniel gave me the booth side, and I stored our coats and hats next to me on the bench seat.

I scanned the crowded room. The din of so many conversations reminded me of cicadas in July.

Daniel glanced around the room. "Wow, I don't think this place is this crowded during lunchtime on a normal business week."

I followed his gaze. "I don't go out for lunch often, but I think you're right."

"What do you normally do for lunch?"

"If I remember to eat, I eat at my desk."

"Sounds like you are working too hard."

"Yes, I have been recently told something along those lines."

He gave me a wary look, and didn't comment further.

The server arrived, saving us both from an awkward moment.

"Do you know what you want?"

Daniel gave me a questioning look. "Do you trust me?"

"Implicitly," I lied.

"Two Surry Burgers with fries."

"And to drink?"

"Two coffees and two waters."

"You got it." Her eyes never left her order pad. She hurried to the next table. I thought she must be struggling to keep up with the crowd.

"Is it always this busy?"

"No, I'm mean they are full at lunchtime, but not like this. It's popular because the service is superb here, and the food is even better."

The server returned with the coffee and water. I was impressed that she successfully maneuvered the tray loaded with liquid through the narrow aisles and in between all the people. That took skill, but to be honest, she looked like she had been doing it for a while.

Daniel leaned forward a little to be heard over the din of the crowd. "So, how's the plans for this weekend going?"

"Good. I walked by the site on the way here and I've talked to the audio people. They assure me they will be here Saturday in a mobile unit on site to ensure it all goes according to plan here and online."

"That's great. Sounds like it is all coming together."

"I think it really is, and you know what I realized this morning," He leaned back and cocked an eyebrow, "Even if it doesn't go off perfectly this weekend, I did everything I could to make it happen and some things are out of my control." I said, pride creeping into my voice.

"Wow, that sounds like a pretty big revelation. What brought that on?"

I longed to blame him; to tell him it was solely his fault. That because I couldn't control the budget as much as I wanted to, I had learned to let some things go. But I couldn't do that. The blame lies with me. "My friend Christina likes to give me a reality check once in a while."

"Is that a good thing?" He asked in a tone that said he wasn't so sure.

"Yes, I have to be open to hearing her sometimes, and I

have learned that I am not always listening when I should be." I sipped coffee to stop myself from saying more.

"As long as she doesn't hurt your feelings."

His comment surprised me. My initial reaction was to wonder why he cared about my feelings. But I kept my mouth shut. Maybe he was a nice guy and cared about other people that way.

"Sometimes I am too caught up in what I am doing. Sometimes I forget about the rest of the world, and some have labeled me a perfectionist."

"That means you care about what you are doing. And I think you want this event to be the best for the city and not for you personally."

I blinked at his insight into my character. "Do you think so?"

"Yes, of course."

"It's true. I was given this task, and I want to make sure it's the best it can be for everyone and that I give my best effort."

"You need to give yourself a break. Everyone knows how passionate you are."

"Do they?"

He chuckled. "I think your friend may have a slight point. You don't realize how others see you."

Our food arrived in time to save me from what was going to be an embarrassing conversation involving me blushing, which I had no desire to do in front of Daniel.

The burger filled the entire plate. Cole slaw and BBQ sauce was dripping off the burger. This was going to be messy, and there was no delicate way to eat it. I wanted to ask for a fork and knife, but the server had already moved to the next customer.

"What's wrong?" Daniel asked.

"This is messy. I was going to ask for silverware to eat it."

"You are going to cut up a perfectly good burger?"

"Yes."

"Why?" He looked scandalized.

"Because I didn't want to sit across from you with all of this dripping down my chin."

"That is half the fun!" With that, he picked up his burger and took a bite, BBQ falling out from between the buns. I had to laugh until he said, "Your turn."

I shrugged and picked up the burger, taking a small bite to minimize the need for additional napkins, which magically appeared on the table while I was chewing. Daniel laughed.

"That's cheating!"

"How so?"

"Just embrace it. There is no avoiding being messy!"

He was using the napkins liberally. I couldn't remember the last time I had a burger this good. Holding it with one hand, afraid if I put it down, it would all fall apart, and I snagged a fry with the other.

"Now you're getting the hang of it." Daniel encouraged me.

"How are things going on in the budget office?"

"Well, a few last-minute things still need to be wrapped up. No major adjustments are necessary, and we're ready for the next quarter."

"That sounds like a relief. I've never asked if you have enough staff to help you. You don't have to do it all alone, do you?"

He chuckled, "No, I'm not alone. My team consists of five people. But is it ever enough? You know what it's like. There's always have more work than staff."

"That's true!"

The server came back, and this time made eye contact. "Dessert?"

"No, thank you. I couldn't, possibly."

"Same here, thank you, Doretha."

A moment later, Doretha was back with the check. Daniel quickly handed her the cash. "I got this."

"Daniel, let me pay for mine."

"No, I got it." He smiled.

"Thank you, that was sweet."

After we chatted between messy bites and finished our lunch, Daniel stood and then offered his hand to help me slide out from behind the table. Once outside, I took a deep breath of fresh air, enjoying the coolness on my skin for a moment.

"Wow, that place was packed," I said while pulling on my coat.

"Yeah, it's always popular, but I didn't realize it would be quite so popular today. Next time, we'll go someplace a little more relaxed."

I smiled, noting his words 'next time'. "The food was worth it, though. I won't need to eat dinner tonight." I laughed.

"Want to walk off some of that food?" Daniel asked.

"What did you have in mind?"

"How about a change of scenery?"

"Okay." I was a little cautious about what he might have in mind.

He drove us across town, and I was happy the streets had been cleared and treated, which held promise for the tree lighting ceremony. We drove into the old fort, and I was in awe. Most of the snow here in the grassy areas had been untouched. It looked like a perfect winter scene. The parking lot was missing a few spaces because of the piles of snow, but we were the only car, so it didn't matter. We got out. The wind off the water was bracing. The waves were choppy.

I stood next to the car, taking it all in.

Daniel's voice broke the spell. "What are you doing?"

"I don't want to disturb the snow. It is so beautiful." I breathed.

"Hmm, okay." He looked around. "Wait here."

He walked in the street. "Okay then, hold my hand in case it gets slippery." No cars passed by; no one ventured out in these temperatures. From the street, the water remained visible beyond a small field of snow separating us from the seawall. We walked to the next parking lot, which someone had cleared. Standing at the edge, we gazed out at the water, momentarily oblivious to Daniel's presence. It was all so beautiful.

"Harper, you're shivering. Maybe we should go back."

"It is so peaceful here."

"I know, but I don't want you to get too cold."

"I'm fine."

He chuckled. "Okay, a few more minutes, then we need to walk again to get the blood circulating."

I nodded. Now that he had mentioned the cold. My teeth started chattering. I felt Daniel's arm around my shoulder.

"Come on, we need to warm you up."

I shoved my gloved hands into my coat pockets. We started walking back to the car when I thought I heard something. I stopped.

"What is it?"

"Shh, I hear something."

We stood, not moving, my ears straining to hear a sound. I was about to chalk it up to my imagination when I heard it again.

"Did you hear that?" I asked.

"I think so. What is it?"

"I'm not sure, an animal or a child?" I took a step forward and listened again.

Daniel pointed, "that way, I think."

My thoughts of keeping the snow pristine were gone. We

trudged across the street towards the moat. Then we stopped and listened again. Daniel was right. The sound came again and this time I could tell it was a cat. I looked around, trying to pinpoint the location, but we were closer now. We moved cautiously, and I called out.

"Here, kitty, kitty, kitty. Where are you?"

More mewing. I kept calling and listening we walked around slowly.

"Over by the tree!" I cried; Spotting a little gray fur ball under a tree. I rushed over and scooped it up. It was a tiny little kitten, half frozen.

"It's so small, it shouldn't be out here alone." Daniel began looking around. "Do you think there are others?"

Taking off my gloves, I began inspecting the kitten for injury. I didn't see any obvious signs that it had been hit by a car or attacked by something larger.

"I think I found the momma," Daniel said. "She looks hurt."

Daniel scooped up a dark gray cat that looked limp to me. I held my breath. Daniel nestled her inside his coat, and I did the same with the kitten. "Are there anymore?" I asked.

"I don't think so, but let's look around for a few more minutes."

We walked around, searching for any signs of other kittens. Daniel got down on his hands and knees, brushing snow away from where we'd found the mother cat. Concern gnawed at me as I considered the possibility that the mother had moved her babies, leaving some abandoned elsewhere. Without tracks in the snow, it was impossible to tell where they might have come from. I strained to hear any sounds of more kittens, but all I heard was the trees creaking under the weight of the snow and the wind whistling through the branches.

"Harper, I don't think we are going to find any more and this one needs a vet."

"Okay." I nodded reluctantly. I hated the thought of leaving helpless kittens out here in this weather. But we couldn't let the ones we found die while looking for others.

Hurrying back to the car, Daniel turned the heat on full blast. I took the cat from Daniel so he could drive and put her inside my coat with her baby. We rushed as best we could to the emergency vet.

We sat in the waiting room with several other people, silently. A technician came out and invited us back into one of the exam rooms.

"I'm Dr. Miller."

"Harper Wade,"

"Daniel Stewart."

"Where did you say you found the cat and kitten?"

"They were half buried in the snow out at Ft. Monroe." I answered, wringing my hands.

"It is a good thing you found them when you did."

"Will they be alright?" Daniel asked.

"They kitten will recover. The mother isn't out of the woods yet. We'd like to keep her overnight." Dr. Miller looked from Daniel to me. "What are your plans for them? Are you going to take them to a shelter?"

I had given little thought to what would happen after I had been so focused on making sure they were okay. "No, I will take them home with me."

Daniel shot me a look.

"I mean, unless you wanted to adopt them," I added quickly.

Daniel nodded. "We can work it out later. What matters is that they both have homes to go to."

"Exactly." I agreed.

The vet smiled, "the kitten will be ready in about thirty

minutes. If you leave your contact information with the staff out front, we will call to give you an update on the momma cat tomorrow."

We nodded and went back out to the waiting room.

"Did you want to adopt one of them?" I asked Daniel.

"Well, if you don't mind, I like to take the momma cat home."

"I don't mind at all. I'm sure she will pull through." Trying to offer him a bit of comfort.

Daniel looked back at the exam room door. "I hope so. No telling how long they were out in those temperatures and what kind of life they had before."

I reached over and squeezed his hand, and then pulled it back quickly.

After another thirty minutes, we paid the bill for the kitten, and I bought some kitten food. I put her back in my coat and Daniel drove us home.

"What will you do for a litter box?"

"I'll go to the store tomorrow. Tonight, I will spread some paper into a foil pan."

Daniel nodded. "Do you know what you are going to name him?"

"Not yet. I think I will see what his personality is before I stick him with a name."

Daniel laughed, "I wouldn't expect anything less."

CHAPTER 13

Daniel

I drove home, thinking about how the day had unfolded. Nothing had gone as planned, starting with the overcrowded restaurant, which ruined my plans for a quiet lunch so I could get to know Harper better, to ending up in a veterinary clinic. It wasn't at all how I'd imagined things would go, but I was quickly learning that nothing with Harper ever went as planned.

For every step forward in building a relationship with her, it felt like we took two steps back. The moment she had grasped my hand at the vet and her desire to find and save kitten and momma cat made me fall even more in love with her.

I thought about how long those cats had been outside. Despite never intending to have a pet, I couldn't let them remain homeless after a near-death experience. I imagined Harper sleeping with her new fuzzy friend curled up beside her and sighed. That momma cat and I had a few things in common. We were both left in the cold, and we were both alone tonight. I turned around and drove back to the emergency vet.

"Can I help you?"

"Yes, I was here earlier with my friend, and I brought in a kitten and a momma cat. The momma cat is still here."

"Your name?"

"Daniel Stewart."

"Yes, Mr. Stewart, I found you in the system. What can I do for you?"

"I know the cat is under observation tonight. I wonder if I could sit with her."

The technician smiled, "Let me ask." she got up and walked to the back.

I looked around the waiting room. There were fewer people waiting in the hard plastic chairs than earlier in the evening.

"Mr. Stewart, you can come back."

I followed the Tech through the door. I looked around at the treatment and recovery area. Several steel wall cages housed patients. I noticed another tech standing near an open cage with an IV hanging off the door.

"This is Kristin, our manager."

The tech disappeared. Kristin turned to face me. "She's hanging in, but she is severely dehydrated. There appears to be frost bite on her left front paw. We are hoping we don't have to amputate."

"Amputate!" I rushed over to look in the cage.

A needle in her front leg with gauze wrapped around it to hold it in place. Her were eyes closed, and her fur was still ruffled.

"Do you think she will be alright?"

"It is still a little touch and go. There aren't any broken

bones, although the x-ray shows she has in the past. She is probably feral and may not be too happy when she wakes up."

"Feral?" I whispered. "Can I stay with her, so she isn't alone?"

Kristin smiled, "Sure." Stepping away, and I took her place and stroked the cat's fur. "What a rough life you have had," I whispered.

Kristin returned with a stool for me to sit on. "If she wakes up, shut the cage door for safety reasons. We don't want her trying to escape and ripping out her IV."

"Right." I nodded. Once I was seated, I continued to stroke her fur and talk to her. I wasn't sure if it was the same as talking to a human in a coma, but I was going to try, anyway. No one deserved to be left alone like this. And I had no idea what would happen to her if I didn't adopt her. I would cover her medical expenses and give her a good home. She deserved to be treated better.

After a while, Kristin came back to check on me and the cat. I assured her we were both fine. She left the treatment room and disappeared into an office. I must have dozed off for a minute. I came awake with something warm rubbing against my hand. As I opened my eyes, I saw a dark gray head bumping my hand, asking for more pets.

"Hey, little one." I stroked her head. "How are you feeling?" The cat looked groggy. At least, I think she did. I had no idea what a groggy cat looked like. Her eyes were glassy, and I suspected she was still under the influence of whatever medication they had given her. She purred a little and then laid back down. I kept petting her and whispering to her until Kristin came back to check on her.

"How is she doing?"

"She woke up for a minute and purred a little."

"Well, that can be a good sign."

I moved out of the way to let her examine the cat. I had been waiting, thinking I needed to come up with a name for her. If she made it through the night, I promised myself I would give her a name. Now it looked like I needed to think of one.

"Mr. Stewart?"

"Yes?" Kristin's voice brought back to the present. "We need to wait for the vet to examine your cat this morning, but I think she did a great job surviving the night and you should be able to take her home today."

I sighed in relief; I didn't realize how anxious I had been until she told me things were going to be okay. "That's great news, thank you!"

"She is going to be out of it for a little while longer, but she is out of the woods. If you want to go grab some coffee, we'll call you when she is ready to go home."

"Yes, thank you. That's great." I felt like I was walking on air back to my car. Before texting Harper and sharing the good news, I planned on grabbing a cup of coffee and finding an open store to purchase some cat supplies. I knew Nick had some things at the hardware store, like collars and travel crates.

I pulled into the parking lot as Nick was unlocking the front door.

"You're out early," he said in greeting.

"Yeah, I guess so." I followed him into the store.

"What are you looking for? You don't have a burst pipe, do you?"

"No, no, nothing like that. I need some cat supplies."

Nick looked at me incredulously. "Cat supplies?"

"Yeah, I found a cat last night half frozen in the snow. Well, actually it was two cats and Harper was there, but the point is we took them to the vet and Malin survived the night, so I am going to take her home."

"Wait," Nick held up his hands, "Whose Malin and why was Harper at the veterinary clinic?"

"Malin is what I am going to name the cat. It means little warrior."

Nick shook his head. "Dude, have you been drinking?"

"What? No."

Nick took a step closer and stared at me. "Did you hit your head on the ice or something?"

"Stop! I am fine. Harper and I went out to lunch yesterday." I ignored the look on Nick's face. "We went out to the fort for a walk afterwards and we found a momma cat and one of her kittens in the snow. They were cold as ice and the momma cat, has frost bite on one of her paws. So, we took them to the emergency vet."

"And you are adopting them?"

"Only the momma cat, the kitten, was fine, and Harper took him home last night."

"Harper?"

"Yes, Harper." Frustrated with Nick's questions, I tried to change the subject. "I need a collar, a little box, a travel crate, and some food. Do you have any of that?"

"Yeah, man. I got all that." Nick grinned.

"Okay, good."

Nick led the way to the pet aisle, and I picked up two small bowls, a collar with a bell on it, a little pan. "I'll carry the litter." Nick said as he hoisted the back up onto his shoulder.

"So, aside from rescuing two cats from the cold, how did the date go with Harper?"

"Well, we had a wonderful lunch at Midtown Eats and then went for a walk along the water before we rescued the cats. Then we spent half the night at the emergency vet. Well, Harper did. I went back after I took her and the kitten home."

"You went back to the emergency clinic?"

"I couldn't stop thinking about that cat being left to die in the snow, and then dropped off at a veterinary hospital.

Nick paused while placing my supplies into a small cardboard box. "You're a good man, Daniel."

"Thanks," I muttered. I carried the box and the bag of litter out to my car and put them in the trunk. My phone started buzzing, and I rushed to answer it, thinking it would be the emergency clinic.

"Hello?"

"Daniel, it's Harper. I was wondering if there was any news about the momma kitty yet."

"Oh hey, Harper. Just waiting for the vet to come in and reexamine her, but they think she might go home today. She has frost bit on one paw, but they are hoping she won't lose it. I'm at the hardware store picking up supplies, so I'll be ready to take her home."

"Oh, I am sorry about the frostbite. What are they going to do?"

"I guess they are waiting for the vet to look at it to determine if they have to amputate or not."

"Oh, that is terrible."

"Yeah, I'm hoping it's not that bad."

"You're at Nick's store?"

"Yeah, just leaving. Wanna meet for coffee?"

"Sure, where?"

"Your mom's shop?"

"See you soon."

Harper hung up before I could ask how her kitten was doing. I got in the car and drove over to the bakery. I arrived as Harper was sitting down. She looked up when the bell on the door rang.

Her mom greeted me. "Good morning, Daniel. Coffee?"

"Good morning, yes, please."

I joined Harper at the table, where she was still standing. I heard a soft mewing.

"Good morning. Did you bring the kitten with you?"

"Of course, I couldn't leave him all alone." She picked up a bag with mesh sides and started talking to the kitten.

I laughed, "where did you find that so early in the morning?"

"Those big box stores open early."

"Have you decided on a name?"

"Yeti." She smiled and reached in and brought out the fluffiest kitten I'd ever seen.

"Hi, Yeti." I said, petting his head. She was white with gray points and wearing a diamond collar. "It's clear that you're already spoiling him," I said, while petting his head.

"Harper, put that cat back in the carrier."

"Mom, he's fine."

"It's been living on the streets, no telling what it has."

"He got shots last night. He's probably healthier than half of your regular customers."

"Harper Lynn, put that cat away or I will not bring you breakfast."

Harper's face reddened, and I could tell she was embarrassed about being scolded.

I gave her a sympathetic smile.

Her mom came over with the coffee, but Harper refused to look at her. Judy walked away without further comment.

"How did he do over night?" I tried changing the subject.

"Great. He was starving and then slept on the pillow next to me all night. I didn't get any sleep, though."

"Yeah, me either. I went back to the clinic and stayed all night with Malin."

"Malin?"

"That is what I am going to name the momma kitty."

"That is a beautiful name. Why did you pick that one?"

"It means little warrior."

"Oh, that is perfect."

"Yeah, I thought so."

"Wait, so you have been up all night? Why didn't you call me? I would have sat with you."

"Thanks, I appreciate that. But I wanted to keep Malin company. I promised myself if she lived through the night, I'd name her and take her home."

Harper got an odd look on her face, and then she smiled. "You're so sweet."

I shifted in my chair. "Yeah, well...."

Judy reappeared, saving me from an awkward moment.

"You kids want breakfast?"

Harper was apparently still stinging from her mom's comment. "Nothing for me, thanks."

"Daniel?"

"I'm good with coffee for now."

"Let me know if you change your mind."

We drank our coffee, and then I leaned over. "Are you hungry?"

Harper looked at me, and I could tell she was trying to decide how to answer the question.

"I was craving pancakes." I offered her an out.

"I'd love pancakes." She whispered.

I pulled out some bills. "Thank you, Ms. Wade, but I have to go."

"You're leaving already?"

"Yeah, I need to go check on the other cat." I waved. Harper followed me out.

"Harper, where are you going?" Judy called out.

"Taking Yeti home. I have a tree lighting ceremony tonight."

"Okay, talk to you later."

Harper turned to me. "Meet you at the Pancake Hut."

"See you then."

CHAPTER 14

Daniel

I checked my phone to make sure I didn't have any messages from the emergency clinic before walking into the Pancake Hut. I got a table and waited for Harper. Knowing I'd crash hard soon if the caffeine wore off, I ordered coffee.

Harper arrived a few minutes later without Yeti. "Thanks for this."

"No worries, you can only eat so many croissants and bagels, right?"

"Exactly."

The server appeared with coffee for Harper and a menu.

"I think I am in the mood for blueberry pancakes." She gave her order to the server without looking at the menu.

"With bacon?"

"Yes, please."

The server turned to me. "Plain pancakes for me, please."

"Excellent choice. I'll be back." She turned and left.

Turning to Harper, "What can I do to help you tonight?"

"Nothing. I am as ready as I can be."

I laughed. "That's great!"

"The mayor is going to throw the ceremonial switch, so fingers crossed that goes off without a hitch."

We both laughed. But I could see she was nervous about tonight. "Do you want me to come with you, you know, for moral support?" I asked, hoping she would say yes, and I wouldn't feel like a fool.

"Are you sure you want to do that? I mean, it might not be much fun."

"I'm sure I'll manage, besides the goal for tonight is to make sure it's great for the citizens, right?"

"Yeah, you're right." She smiled. "It would be great if you could be there."

My phone rang. The number of the veterinary clinic appeared on the screen.

"Excuse me, it's the clinic. Hello?"

"Mr. Stewart, this is Dr. Miller calling about your cat." I looked up at Harper and she mouthed the word 'vet', and I nodded. She sat, nibbling on her lower lip, which would have been endearing if I wasn't focused on the vet's words.

"Except for the frostbite, she is in remarkable shape, all things considered."

"What does that mean except the frostbite?"

"I'm afraid she will lose a toe."

"But not her whole paw, right?"

"That is correct. The damage to the paw wasn't as severe as I had originally feared. She will lead a normal life. I need your consent to do the surgery. You should still be able to take her home later today."

"Okay, yes, please do the surgery." The doctor said goodbye, and I hung up.

Harper leaned forward. "How's Malin?"

"One of her toes has to be removed because of the frostbite. At least it isn't the whole paw. Thank goodness."

Harper leaned back and blew out a small breath. "That is a relief."

"Yeah, the vet says, I can still pick her up later today. I hope it is early before the ceremony."

Harper reached out and covered my hand with hers. "Hey, Malin comes first. If you have to miss the ceremony to go get her and take her home, that is completely understandable."

"Thanks, I'll hope for the best." It was soft and warm, and I liked the way it felt. Harper looked at it too and jerked it away quickly and put it in her lap.

"Sorry." She muttered.

"Don't be. I like it."

She looked up at me, and I could see it in her eyes. Her mind had gone somewhere else. Was it an old boyfriend, someone that had broken her heart? It made me angry to think about someone hurting her. I didn't want to pressure her; I had a feeling that would only push her away further.

She looked around for the server. "I should probably get going. I'm afraid to think about what Yeti might be doing in my apartment unsupervised."

I laughed, "Go on, I'll take care of the check."

"No, absolutely not. You paid for lunch yesterday. I can at least pay for breakfast." She flagged the server with her credit card in hand. I caught myself staring at her with a smile on my face. She was such a different person than the Harper I knew from the budget meetings. If you had told me a couple of weeks ago, the person I knew then as Harper Wade would spend her time braving the cold to search for stranded kittens in the snow, I wouldn't have believed it. Now I knew her as a completely different person. It made me appreciate the tough exterior she used at work to get things done.

With the bill paid, and two coffees to go, I walked her to her car and promised to call later and let her know how Malin was doing.

I took the supplies home and set up everything in my bedroom and put the litter box in my upstairs bathroom. I didn't want her to have to go far, and I shredded some paper and put it in the litter box.

Later in the afternoon, the vet called to let me know Malin was ready to come home. She was still a little groggy when the tech placed her in the carrier. The vet reminded me I'd need to follow up in a few days to check her incision and ensure everything was healing properly.

I sat her carrier next to the fluffy cat bed I'd set up for her, with food and water nearby. I sat for a while, reluctant to leave her alone in the unfamiliar surroundings. She was still groggy and didn't stray far from the bed.

As the time for the tree lighting ceremony approached, I remembered my promise to Harper. After giving Malin a few gentle pets, I reluctantly left.

Once I arrived at the park in the central district, I sent Harper a quick text. "I'm here, Harper. Where are you?"

"I'm near the Christmas tree. I'll meet you at the stage."

I waited for several minutes before Harper showed up.

"Hey, sorry. Thanks for coming."

"I wouldn't miss it."

"How's Malin?"

"Resting comfortably at home."

"That's good. I'd like to come visit her sometime, if that is, okay?"

"Of course." My heart flipped. Maybe Harper was relaxing more around me. I would have to give Malin an extra treat for the assistance.

"So, is everything on track? You good to go for tonight?"

"As ready as I'll ever be."

"It will be fine. It's going to be an amazing show this year." I smiled at her for encouragement.

"Hope so. Between the weather and the budget, I wasn't so sure."

I looked at her for a moment.

"Oh Daniel, I'm sorry I didn't mean…"

"I get it."

"I know if it were up to you, we'd have all the money in the world for this."

I smiled, so maybe she was coming around to seeing things my way. Or at least understanding the reasons I couldn't give her all the money for the budget she requested.

"Oh, I'm sorry Daniel, I have to run."

"Go have fun."

She turned and disappeared. I strolled over to a beverage stand and ordered a hot chocolate, no point in not embracing the festive atmosphere. I walked towards the Christmas village that I had helped build while keeping the tree and the stage in view. Regardless of my relationship with Harper, if you could call it that, I didn't want to miss the tree lighting.

I thought I saw Nick and Judy in the crowd, but a voice came over the loudspeakers and I turned my attention towards the stage. I saw camera flashes.

The mayor's voice led the countdown to the tree lighting. "5…,4…,3…,2…1 Merry Christmas!"

The tree lit up from bottom to top, ending with the star, as music began to play. The show lasted fifteen minutes, and we were then told there would be a fifteen-minute intermission before the next show, at which time the lights would change colors, and the music would have a different Christmas theme.

The snow added to the atmosphere of the event, and it hadn't lessened the crowds in my opinion. After sipping my hot chocolate and watching the next show on the tree, I started strolling among the vendors. I checked my phone, but there were no messages from Harper. Tonight was her big night, and I was sure she didn't need me to keep her company. So, I text her before heading home to check on Malin.

"Congratulations, went off without a hitch."

I didn't get an immediate response, so I walked back to the parking lot when I heard Nick's voice.

"Hey Daniel!"

"Hey, man."

Nick walked over with Judy on his arm. Seeing them together made me happy for both of them. "Where're you headed? You're not leaving, are you?"

"Yeah, actually I was."

"Join us for dinner."

I looked around, "Not vendor food, I hope?"

"No, actually, we were going across town. You know, get away from the crowds a bit."

"That sounds good. What did you have in mind?"

"The Seabreeze,"

"Perfect. I haven't been there in a while. I'll meet you there."

"See ya, soon."

Walking back to the car, wondering if I had time to run home and check on Malin, then I wondered about my sanity. I was seriously considering going home to check on a cat instead of meeting Nick for seafood and beer. What was wrong with me? The fact that I was contemplating using the cat as an excuse to stay home was a clear sign I needed to get out more.

I drove across town to the waterfront. The parking lot of the Seabreeze was only half full. I waited outside on the deck for Nick and Judy. I wished Harper was joining us, but knew she would be busy late into the night with the ceremony.

Nick and Judy arrived. We didn't have to wait for a table and practically had the waterfront dining room to ourselves.

Our server appeared right away, and I ordered a beer.

"I thought the show was excellent this year." Judy said as soon as the server left.

"Yeah, it was," Nick and I agreed.

I immediately felt awkward, like I was the third wheel and was having second thoughts about being here. Maybe I should have gone home to my cat, which was totally pathetic.

Judy smiled. "Harper says you had a hand in her adopting that kitten?"

"Well, I helped her rescue it. I had nothing to do with her deciding to keep it."

"Rescued, do you mean literally?" Judy asked, "When she said she rescued it, I thought she meant from a shelter or something."

"No, she meant it literally. We went walking in the snow out at Ft. Monroe and she heard it meowing. Then we tracked it down and found a kitten and its momma half frozen in the snow."

Judy gasped. "Oh, no!"

"We picked them up and tried to get them warm and then drove to the emergency vet. The kitten was in much better shape than the momma."

Judy leaned in. "What happen to the momma kitty?"

"She had frostbite on one of her paws and had to have a toe removed. So, she stayed overnight at the vet, but I brought her home earlier today." I glanced at Nick. He had mentioned none of this to Judy, evidently.

"Oh, that is so sweet of you." Judy clutched her chest.

"I couldn't just abandon her."

"You are such a sweet man." Judy smiled.

I wasn't sure if I was sweet or not, but it seemed like the logical thing to do, and I would not leave any animal stranded or in need of help. I could only hope Harper felt the same way.

CHAPTER 15

❄

Nick

December 5th

The tree lighting ceremony marked the true beginning of the holiday season, even though the stores had been decorated for months. I'd held off on putting out the Christmas stock until after Halloween, and once they were displayed in November, the decorations flew off the shelves. Still, it hadn't felt like Christmas to me—until tonight. With the fresh snowfall, the huge Christmas tree glowing, and walking hand-in-hand with Judy under the twinkling lights strung between the light poles, hot cider in hand, it was absolute perfection. For the first time, I truly felt the holiday spirit, as if it were already Christmas Day.

Judy was everything I admired, kind, caring, honest, and determined. As I watched her lean in, listening closely to

Daniel's story about the cat he'd rescued from the snow, her compassion was obvious. She reached out to gently touch his arm, her eyes filled with warmth and encouragement. It was impossible not to feel the quiet strength behind her kindness, a strength that drew people in and made them feel seen.

I noticed he checked his phone a couple of times and then gave up.

The server came back to offer us dessert.

"We have peppermint cheesecake, fried snowballs, hot fudge brownie….,"

"What is a fried snowball?" I asked.

The server leaned over and whispered, "Don't let Chef know I told you, but it's a secret recipe - fried vanilla ice cream with nuts and chocolate sauce."

I nodded. "Well, now I absolutely have to try that."

The server nodded and looked at Judy. "Oh, cheesecake, no question."

"None for me, thanks," Daniel looked at the two of us, "I should be going."

The server repeated our order and left.

I was a little worried about Daniel. "You okay to drive, man?"

"Yeah, I'll be fine. I drank plenty of water too, and those were light beers." He gave me a halfhearted smile. "I need to go check on Malin."

When we both gave him a questioning look, he said, "The cat."

"Oh," Judy said, reaching over for his hand. "I'm so glad you came with us tonight and I wish you didn't have to go, but I understand."

Daniel smiled at her and left.

I have to admit, as much fun as Daniel is to have around normally, I was glad for some more alone time with Judy. I couldn't resist the urge to keep her close and not share her with anyone. All I wanted was to sit and stare into her eyes, losing myself forever. Which is strange for me, but the feelings were so strong I couldn't ignore them.

I drove Judy home and walked her to the door.

"Would you like to come in?" Her voice a little husky.

"Yes, I would. Just don't know if I should." I said, leaning down to kiss her.

I could feel her smile against my lips as she pushed opened the door and grabbed the front of my coat to pull me in. She nearly stumbled, and I scooped her up and carried her inside despite her squeals of protest. I put her down in the living room, both of us laughing.

"What are you doing? You can't carry me like that."

"Yes, I can. And I just did."

"I can't remember the last time anyone picked me up like that, but I am sure it was before I had children." She gasped, out of breath from laughing.

"Well, then I haven't treated you like the queen you are, and I will change that," I said, taking a step closer and elevating the seriousness of the situation once again. She blushed slightly, and I ran my index finger down her cheek to her chin and lifted it gently so I could kiss her.

She wrapped her arms around me and returned the kiss, allowing it to grow passionately. I wanted nothing more than to carrying her upstairs to her bedroom. But I didn't want to rush her.

"Judy,"

She pulled back a little. "Yes?"

"Maybe we should slow down a little."

She took a step back and searched my face. "I'm sor…"

"No." I cupped her face in my hands. "It's not like that at all. So do not apologize. I don't want to pressure you. I want you to feel comfortable."

Judy smiled. "So you're not attracted to me?"

I smiled, "I am so very attracted to you, Judy Wade."

"I'm glad," she whispered. "I am attracted to you."

She took my hand and tugged me towards the stairs. I didn't move, uncertain if the time was right.

She looked back at me again. "Something wrong?"

"Not at all. Well, just one thing."

"What's that?"

"This," I held up our hands. She looked at me, confused. I swept her off her feet and headed for the stairs. "That's better."

"You're incorrigible."

"Better you know now." I chuckled as I carried her up the stairs and to her bedroom.

I scanned the room before placing Judy down on the bed. "I want this to be special."

She smiled up at me, "it will be special because you are special, nothing else matters."

My heart flipped over a few times and then I spent the rest of the night trying my hardest to make sure Judy would still think I was still special in the morning.

When I woke up, I was alone. Looking around the room and then towards the bathroom. No Judy. I had a moment of panic, then the scent of coffee filled the air. I got up and dressed. Judy was in the kitchen, of course, making breakfast.

I came up behind her and wrapped one arm around her, kissing the top of her head, "Morning,"

She turned into me, "Morning, handsome."

I kissed her again. "What are you doing?"

"I was going to bring you breakfast in bed, but how can I when you're up and dressed?"

"Oh no! If anyone deserves to be treated to breakfast in bed it, is you."

"Stop talking nonsense. Grab some coffee and sit down."

"Judy, you don't have to wait on me. Let me wait on you for once."

She looked at me like I was crazy for a minute. "It's been a long time since anyone waited on me or wanted to."

"Well, we will not worry about the past anymore. From now on, it is only the present and the future."

She kissed me as she sat a plate of food in front of me. "Okay, for now. Eat your breakfast."

I laughed, "Yes, ma'am."

The morning was sharp with cold air—colder than any December in years. Once at the store, I flipped on the office TV to catch the weather report. Snow was coming again, and I ran through the aisles, taking quick stock: shovels, winter gloves, kerosene heaters. I checked the schedule to see who'd be on shift and thought about whether I'd have time to swing by Judy's for lunch. Flowers might be a nice touch. As the sun edged over the horizon, the employees started trickling in, filling the place with the hum of morning routine—coffee in hand, ready to go. Much as I liked the quiet before opening, that first burst of energy felt just as good.

The day got busy, and it became obvious that I wouldn't be able to get away to surprise Judy at lunchtime, so I ordered flowers online and scheduled a delivery by the end of the day.

CHAPTER 16

❄

Harper

The tree was lit, the mayor and council members had made their speeches, and had rejoined their families in the VIP tent for the festivities. I wandered around, enjoying the event as a citizen rather than an employee—and I definitely needed something hot to drink. As I strolled through the crowd, I took in the sight of kids skating on the ice rink, people enjoying the light show, and families taking pictures. I felt tempted to text Christina to see if she was still here, but I savored a few more minutes of solitude. We had all worked so hard on this project, and although the snow had initially seemed like a challenge, it ended up being the perfect backdrop. Plus, we saved money by not needing the snow machines.

The ceremony had gone flawlessly—no technical glitches, an enormous crowd, and a strong online turnout as well. I was already thinking ahead to next year, making a mental note to incorporate live streaming in the future, regardless of the weather. I'd need to jot down notes for the follow-up meeting at work, but I also wanted to keep my ideas fresh for next year.

Mom had texted to say everything looked great, and that she and Nick were enjoying the hot chocolate and cider stand. I was starting to accept the idea of my mother dating someone—and it didn't feel as strange as I thought it would.

The light shows ended at ten o'clock, so I walked over to the control booth to make sure everything was secure for the night. It has been a blast, but I was cold and ready to go home and snuggle with Yeti for a week, except the city offices were reopening tomorrow, so I had to go to work in the morning.

I checked my phone and noticed the battery was dead. Great.

By the time I got home, I was so cold I was numb, hungry and tired. Yeti met me at the door. The volume of his meowing suggested he was also famished.

"Okay, okay. I left you crunchies. Did you eat them?" I shed my boots, coat, and hat to check out his food situation. There was a small dent in the crunchies, and he had plenty of water. Grabbing his bowl from the dish drain, I added some pate kitten food and presented it to him. He sniffed it as it giving it his approval and then devoured the food.

"Good, you eat. I'm going to take a hot shower." Clothes were peeled off on the way to the bathroom, which quickly filled with steam. Lingering under the spray, waiting for my bones to thaw, I enjoyed the warmth. Afterward, heavy sweats and fuzzy socks were a must. Yeti was sound asleep in the middle of the bed. So I padded to the kitchen and pulled out everything I need to make mac and cheese. It took a while, but the effort was worth it in the end. Curled up on the sofa, I turned on a holiday romance movie and ate until I was full.

I woke up to Yeti trying to sleep on my head and sunlight streaming into the room. Sunlight? Jumping up, I searched for my phone, eventually finding it in my coat pocket, still uncharged. The clock in the kitchen showed eight o'clock, and the offices were opening two hours late. There was still time to get ready.

Putting my phone on the charger, I prepared Yeti's breakfast and topped off his crunchies since anything less than a full to overflowing bowl was unacceptable.

I walked into the office a few minutes before ten o'clock, noticing only a handful of people around. A quick glance at my phone showed a text from my mom and two from Christina. Nothing from Daniel.

I opened my mom's message first: "Nick and I are going to dinner with Daniel. Come with us."

Great. They all likely thought I was some kind of snob. I'd call my mom later and explain. Next, I checked Christina's text, asking where I was and if I wanted to walk to the Christmas village with her.

It looked like I was going to spend my morning apologizing to friends and family. I wondered if that was why I hadn't gotten a text from Daniel. Since I didn't join them for dinner, he likely thought I was blowing him off after asking him to come to the ceremony to be my moral support.

I sat down in my chair and sent Christina a text.

"Sorry about last night. My phone was dead, and I didn't realize it. I went home and crashed."

She replied immediately. "Thought you might have escaped as soon as you could."

"Did you talk to Daniel last night or to my mom?"

"No, did you?"

"No. Lunch today?" I asked.

"Yeah, that would be great. Text details later."

Glad that Christina didn't seem to be upset with me, it was time to face my mother. I sent a text, "Hey phone died last night, so I just got your text this morning." I didn't expect an immediate response knowing she was working.

Daniel crossed my mind, but seeking him out at work felt awkward, so I pushed the thought aside and focused on my emails, diving into the tasks that needed attention.

An hour later, my mother sent me a text, "Are you coming for lunch today?"

"Yes, Christina and I will be there."

By one-thirty, I was walking into the bakery breathing in the heavenly smell of muffins and cookies.

"There are my girls!" My mom called out.

"Hi Mom,"

"Hi, Judy."

My mom came to hug us both. "How is work going today? Are you girls busy?"

Christina sank down in a chair. "I am. People are coming in, in droves."

My mom laughed, "I bet. Everyone has had time to read all their books and is ready for new ones. What about you, Harper?"

"No busier than normal, I guess."

"I have chicken and dumpling soup if you girls want some."

"Yes, please." We both answered.

Getting up to help mom, she took that opportunity to grill me about the night before.

"Why didn't you come to dinner?"

"I was so tired, and my phone had died. I didn't realize it until I was home and then I fell asleep without putting it on the charger. If it wasn't for Yeti, I would have overslept and been late for work."

"Yes, Daniel told us the whole story about how you two rescued those cats, literally. It was generous of Daniel to pay for everything."

"Hey, I paid for Yeti's bills. Daniel went to dinner with you guys even after I didn't show up?"

"Yes, of course he did." My mother looked at me funny, "he is allowed, you know. He and Nick are friends."

"God, it feels weird my mother dating someone who is friends with one of my friends."

"Nick is my age." She protested.

"I know,"

Together, we walked the soup back to the table.

"Are you two fussing again?" Christina asked.

"No, I was telling mom, my phone died."

"Oh." Christina tried the soup. "Hmm, delicious."

"I'm weirded out by the thought of double dates with my mom, though."

Christina looked at up me, "Ew."

"Exactly."

My mom spoke up, "First, I don't recall asking you to double date with us and second, you need to have some alone time with Daniel."

Christina and I both raised our eyebrows at her.

My mother blushed, "you know what I mean," and then walked away.

Christina and I giggled for a moment before Christina put in her two cents' worth. "Well, she isn't wrong."

"You too?"

"Well, it is obvious that Daniel is into you, and I know we've been over this before. But you need to open up and date someone."

"Why?" I knew she was right, and I didn't want to be an old spinster, but dating was hard, and guys were only after one thing. Nothing long term and it was exhausting weeding through the ones that were worth getting to know.

"Because you're not my type, and you need to go to the movies with someone other than me once in a while."

"Oh, I didn't realize I was that much of a time suck." I said, slightly offended.

"You know that is not what I meant." Christina put her spoon down. "But it might be fun to double date with you." She gave me a devious smile.

"I don't see you dating anyone seriously."

Christina smiled and returned her attention to her soup.

"Are you?" I leaned forward. "Is there someone you haven't told me about? We are BFFs. How could you be dating someone and not tell me?"

"Who says I'm dating anyone?"

"That look on your face speaks volumes."

"We aren't dating."

"So, there is a 'we'?" My voice was a little louder than I intended.

"Who is this guy? Details, please."

"There are no details. It's just a guy who comes into the library once a week to check-out a book or two and we chat for a while. He's never asked me out on a date and I'm not sure I would go; I mean, we are some real weirdos in there, so I'd have to think long and hard before dating a customer."

"Seriously?"

"Yes. Absolutely."

"Well, he wasn't carrying a machete, was he?" I asked, remembering a time she had told me about a machete wielding customer that wanted to use a computer. The police had to remove him.

"That is a good start." Christina laughed.

After a late lunch, I returned to work and found myself still at my desk long after everyone else had gone home. The quietness of the office registered in the back of my mind, helping me focus as I lost track of time. I was finishing up some emails when a tapping sound on the window caught my attention. Turning around, I saw only my reflection against the darkness outside. Moving closer, I realized the tapping was ice mixed with rain. Great. Walking home was going to be fun.

I looked at the time, and decided it was time to check on my Yeti, the fluff ball. I packed up my laptop and headed for the elevator. The doors opened and Daniel was standing there. My heart flipped and the butterflies in my stomach woke up.

"Evening." He smiled.

"Hey," I stepped in and let the doors closed. "How was work today?" I asked, not sure what else to say.

"Busy, as I assume your day was as well."

I nodded, my mouth dry, and I needed a minute to form words. "It doesn't matter that I work from home. It always feels like I'm busier when I come into the office."

"That's because it's easy for people to walk into your office and interrupt your day when you are here."

He had a point. The elevator reached the lobby, and we both walked outside. Ice immediately pelted me.

"Ug!"

"This is going to create a mess. Let me give you a ride home." He offered as a truck drove by spreading deicer on the roadways.

"I'm not so sure a car is the safest place to be right now." I said, looking around at the ice that was already encasing signs and light poles.

Daniel looked around. "You might be right; I hope they have treated the roads."

"Why not come stay at my place tonight? No sense risking an accident." I heard the words coming from my mouth, but had not actually thought about them first. They seemed to form on their own.

He hesitated for a moment. "I appreciate that, but I don't like leaving Malin."

"I understand. Could a neighbor check on her?" I hated the idea of him driving in this mess. But tomorrow morning wasn't going to be any better.

"I suppose." He hesitated.

"Is your car parked in the garage at least?"

"Yes,"

I smiled, "So, it will be safe overnight."

He looked over this shoulder back at city hall and the parking garage next door. I was shivering, and it felt like the ice was encasing me along with everything else.

"You might be right." He finally said.

I smiled and nodded, "Come on,"

He took my arm as we slipped and slid our way to my apartment. I was never more grateful to live so close to work than tonight. Once inside my apartment, Daniel removed his coat and pulled out his phone. "Excuse me, while I call a neighbor."

I nodded and turned my attention to the abominable fur ball at my feet. "Let's feed you." I picked up Yeti and took him to the kitchen.

"Hi Beth, it's Daniel. Listen, the roads are pretty nasty. I'm going to stay at a friend's tonight. Do you mind checking on Malin for me?"

There was a pause. I focused on opening a can of cat food, trying not to eavesdrop on Daniel's conversation, but curiosity got the best of me. Who was this, Beth? I imagined someone young, with long blond hair and an infectious, sparkling personality. My stomach tightened at the thought. Did she have a key to Daniel's house?

"Well, that's all arranged," Daniel said from the kitchen doorway.

I jumped, "Oh, that's good."

"So, how is this little guy doing?" Daniel stepped over and stroked Yeti's head as the fur ball began purring even louder.

"Oh, he is eating me out of house and home." I laughed.

"He looks bigger than we went found him already." Daniel laughed.

"I know. He grows every day." Daniel was standing so close I had the urge to kiss him. "Hey, listen, I owe you an apology."

He tilted his head, "for what?"

"The other night, at the tree lighting ceremony. My phone died, and I didn't realize it. I got busy, and it was after ten before I left and went home. I didn't get any of the messages until the next day, so everyone thought I was just blowing them off."

He looked sheepish, "Well I will admit I thought it was kinda odd you asked me to come support you and then I didn't hear from you the rest of the night."

"I am really very sorry."

"Thank you. I'm glad weren't brushing me off."

"No, no! Not at all. I'm bummed I missed dinner with you, mom and Nick. It sounds like you guys had a nice time."

"Yeah, it was okay. I felt like a third wheel, so I left early. Besides, I needed to check on Malin."

"How is she doing?"

"She seems fine. I don't think she is feral, maybe a stray, but she had definitely been around people before and knows she prefers to sleep in my bed." He laughed.

"So glad that everything worked out for her."

"I feel bad leaving her alone so much while she is still getting used to things."

"You're such a nice guy." I smiled and patted his chest

more out of instinct, then caught myself. I tried to recover. "Let me cook dinner for you."

"I'm happy to help."

"No way, you're my guest, and it is the least I can do for acting like a jerk. But talk to me while I work?" I asked, feeling like we had turned a corner in the relationship.

"Of course."

I put some chicken in the air fryer and vegetables in the steamer. "We have a few minutes. Want to find a movie to watch?"

"Only if it is a Christmas movie." Daniel grinned.

"Of course!"

CHAPTER 17

❄

Daniel

December 6th

We settled into the sofa, and before I could even get comfortable, Yeti scrambled onto my lap, a gray ball of fluff. He curled up and fell asleep. His purring filled the quiet space.

"Looks like you've made a new friend," Harper said, her voice carrying a warm note that matched her smile.

I looked down at the small creature snoozing contentedly. "It would seem so," I replied, scratching his ears gently. "He's persistent."

"If he's bothering you, I can move him," she offered, her hand hovering near as if she might lift Yeti away.

"No, he's fine." Truth was, I didn't mind. He was a bit of a third wheel, but then again, maybe that was a good thing. I reminded myself this wasn't a date, though the thought lingered.

It was Harper's turn to pick the movie. She selected a Christmas romantic comedy. It wouldn't have been my choice, but he had been a good sport when I picked an action movie the last time we spent the day together. A few minutes in, I grabbed a beer and tried to chuckle in the right spots, though I was more focused on her reactions than the movie itself. Her laughter was bright and genuine, and every time she laughed, I smiled too. Soon I followed the storyline and appreciating why she enjoyed these movies.

A timer beeped from the kitchen, breaking the spell, and she paused the movie. "I'll go check on dinner. Want another beer?"

"No, thanks, maybe later." I gently moved Yeti to the side and stood up, feeling the need to stretch and move around. I wandered to the window and peered outside. Ice and rain. Not a hint of snow, but that was typical here this time of year —wet, gray, and chilly with none of the picture postcard winter charm.

From the kitchen, Harper called out, "Dinner's nearly ready."

I turned, watching her as she moved around the small kitchen, her sleeves rolled up, hair a little tousled. The cozy setting, the faint smell of roasted herbs—it all felt uncomfortable... intimate. Almost like playing house. I couldn't deny it. This was harder than I'd expected. Everything in this scene —the dim lights, the Christmas movie, the dinner for two— had me feeling like I was one wrong move away from slipping into territory I couldn't step back from.

"Can I help with anything?" I asked, taking a step toward the kitchen.

She looked over her shoulder. "Sure, could you set the table?"

"Absolutely." I grabbed the silverware she handed me, feeling the brush of her fingers against mine. Her eyes lingered on mine for just a second longer than usual, and I felt my pulse quicken.

The kitchen was small, the kind where you bump into each other every time you turn around. I realized I was more of a hinderance than a help.

She paused what she was doing and handed me the plates and glassware.

I took them from her smile, following me. It was the kind of smile that could pull a man back from the edge, make him believe in good things again. I set the table, watching her bring out steamed vegetables and then the chicken and arrange them on the small table.

"This smells amazing," I said as we sat down.

"Thank you. I was worried the chicken might be overcooked," she admitted, but she looked pleased as I took a bite and nodded approvingly.

"Superb," I said between bites. "You're a fantastic cook."

She relaxed, a small sigh of relief escaping her. "I'm glad you think so. I was worried it might not be enough."

We fell into a comfortable silence, the clinking of silverware the only sound between us. Every so often, our eyes met over the table, and I felt that familiar tension pulling at me. She offered me seconds, and I found myself full long before I wanted to stop eating—if only to prolong the meal, the company.

When we finished, she moved to clean up, but I stopped her. "Let me do the dishes. You cooked; it's only fair."

She shook her head, laughing softly. "We can share. I have a system—besides, I don't want you getting used to this kind of treatment."

She rinsed while I loaded the dishwasher, our hands brushing as we passed each dish back and forth. I could feel her watching me, and I found myself wishing the dishes would multiply. After we placed the last dish on the rack, we both paused, standing side by side, our eyes meeting in the reflection of the kitchen window.

We returned to the sofa, finding another movie, and though I barely followed the plot, I couldn't help but watch her from the corner of my eye. She stifled a yawn, her head dipping slightly.

"You don't have to stay up to entertain me," I said gently, reaching out to touch her arm. Her skin was warm beneath my hand, and she looked at me, searching.

"I'm just tired," she admitted, trying to hide another yawn.

I smiled. "Go on to bed. I'll be fine here."

She hesitated, then offered, "I'll grab you a pillow and blanket. The sofa pulls out into a bed if you want more space."

"Only if it's no trouble." I started unfolding the sofa bed, trying to act nonchalant as she returned with linens, her movements quick but purposeful.

Once the bed was made, she stood at the edge of the room, looking unsure, as if there was something left unsaid. Then, after a quick goodnight, she slipped down the hall to her room. I stripped down to my t-shirt and boxers, sliding under the blanket, my gaze drifting to the window. Outside, clouds skated across the night sky. For a brief moment, I let myself imagine this wasn't just a passing moment—that maybe, just maybe, this was something worth holding onto.

Sometime in the early morning, I felt a soft weight on my chest and opened my eyes to find Yeti curled up, his tiny body rising and falling with his breaths. The apartment was silent, the kind of quiet that feels sacred, and for a while, I just lay there, enjoying the warmth and stillness.

When I woke again, the sun was streaming through the window, and the smell of coffee drifted from the kitchen.

Harper was standing at the end of the sofa, trying to coax Yeti off me with quiet whispers.

"Good morning," I said, stretching.

"Morning. I didn't mean to wake you."

I shook my head, rubbing the sleep from my eyes. "Not at all. Yeti was an excellent bedmate."

She laughed, the sound filling the space. "Would you like breakfast?"

I looked at her, the warmth in her eyes, the casual way she stood there, suggesting feel like so much more. "Only if you're having some, too."

She grinned. "Deal."

As she turned toward the kitchen, I took the chance to freshen up, finding the toothbrush she'd set out. When I came back, she was bustling in the kitchen, making coffee and something that smelled like heaven.

This time, I let myself believe, just for the morning, that maybe this was the beginning of something real. I imagined waking up like this every morning, having breakfast with Harper would be a wonderful way to start my day, every day.

CHAPTER 18

Harper

December 7th

Daniel had left around ten. We were on liberal leave again from work because of the road conditions. Being that it was Friday, I filled out a leave slip, anticipating a much-needed break of a long weekend, during which I could comfortably stay in my pajamas all day. It was nearly noon when my cell phone rang with a call from Christina.

"Hey, what are you doing today?" Her voice greeted me when I answered.

"Being lazy and watching movies with Yeti, wanna come over?"

"Yeah!"

"Good. See you soon."

Half an hour later, Christina was standing at my door in

her pajamas, a trench coat, and fleece-lined boots. I laughed. "Wow!"

"I thought you said you were being lazy. Why are you dressed? " She said, stepping inside with a tote bag almost as bigger than herself.

She took off her boots and put on the biggest pair of fuzzy slippers. "Now I'm ready for a girl's day."

"Excellent. So, what do you want to drink?"

"Cocoa."

"Perfect. I have marshmallows and peppermint."

We made our drinks and then settled on the sofa for movies and BFF quality time.

"Can you believe this weather? I really hope we have snow for Christmas."

"Honestly, now that the tree lighting is done, I don't care if it snows the rest of the month. I'm seriously considering taking the next three weeks off. I'm exhausted."

"I wish I could take three weeks off! If I have to set up one more display or run another story time, I swear I'm going to scream."

"But you love story time."

"She leaned back on the sofa and sighed; I used to."

"You need a break."

"No kidding."

"Have you talked to Daniel?" She looked at me slyly.

"I have."

"Juicy, tell me more."

"We do work in the same building, you know."

She looked disappointed. "You've only seen him at work?"

"I saw him yesterday at work."

"That's it?"

I couldn't lie to her, "Well, no, not exactly."

She shifted on the sofa to face me. "Spill!"

"Well, I saw him in the elevator as I was leaving work, and

I apologized for having missed dinner with him and my mom and Nick after the ceremony." Christina was looking impatient.

"So, we were chatting. When we walked outside, everything was coated in ice."

"Yeah, yeah?"

"We decided the roads were too dangerous, and he shouldn't drive home, so he stayed over last night."

"What?" Christian practically levitated off the sofa. "You are just now telling me you and Daniel spent the night together?"

"Nothing happened. He slept on the sofa."

"Nothing?"

I laughed, "No nothing. I cooked him dinner, watched movies and drank a couple of beers and then he slept out here and I went to my room."

She was looking at me like I had lost my mind.

"What happened in the morning?"

"I got up first, made coffee. He woke up, showered, and dressed. We had a lovely breakfast, and he went home to the office. And I filled out a leave slip for the day."

"Wow." She sipped her cocoa.

"What?"

"That is a lot of will power, to have a hot guy sleeping on your sofa and not even kiss him?"

"It's not like that. We are just friends."

"I'm not so sure. Have you checked with Daniel on that point?"

"What do you mean?"

"Okay, let's break it down. You like him as a person, right?"

"Yes."

"You think he is good looking?"

I nodded.

"You've been on what, three dates?"

"We haven't been on any dates."

"You guys practically eat every meal together and you rescued cats together. You've been on a date."

"We like the same things."

"Yes, that is how most relationships start." Christina snarked.

"We" I pointed to her, then myself, "like the same things." I quipped.

"Yes, and your relationship with Daniel is even more platonic than ours."

"What does that mean?"

"Did you and Daniel sit up in your PJs watching movies?"

"No, we were fully clothed."

"There you go." She turned back around and picked up the remote.

"What makes you think Daniel is even interested in me?"

"Oh, please!" She restarted the movie.

I sat pretending to watch it while thinking about what she said. Sure, Daniel is good looking, and he had asked me to lunch and breakfast, but I hadn't taken it as a romantic overture. It had all been so casual. Would I want a romantic relationship with Daniel? Or with anyone, for that matter?

He was handsome, but I had disliked him for so long. Despite its unfounded nature, contemplating a romantic relationship would require some time. That was if Daniel was even interested. I had been so rude to him in the past he may not have any interesting in me beyond what we're doing.

The movie ended without me even realizing it.

"Earth to Harper."

"What?"

"Are you hungry?"

"Yeah," Lunch was more of a distraction than anything. I needed to stop thinking about Daniel.

"Wanna order take out?"

"What did you have in mind?" I wasn't in the mood for cooking.

"Hmm, pizza?"

I wrinkled my nose. "Something out of the ordinary. No pizza, no Chinese."

"Okay, I know where you are going with this. Hang on." Christina whipped out her phone. A moment later she found the answer, "aha!"

"What?"

"How about Tandoori?"

"I'm listening." My interest was piqued. I hadn't had Indian food in a while.

Christina handed me her phone with the menu. I clicked on my choices and handed her the phone back. She tapped the screen a few times.

"Okay, done. What shall we do in the meantime?"

At that moment, Yeti appeared and jumped in her lap. "Now you must pet Yeti for an hour, or he'll bug us the rest of the day."

She cooed over him. I rolled my eyes. He was adorable, but he was also a pest at the worst possible moments. It must have been the discussion of food that woke him from his nap. I could only hope he would go back to sleep before our lunch arrived.

My phone buzzed with a text message from Daniel.

"Hi,"

As I stared at the screen. I could feel Christina's eyes on me.

"Hi, did you make it home safely?"

"I did. Thank you again."

"Anytime." I regretted the word as soon as I hit sent. It

was an automatic response, but considering Christina's observations earlier, I now felt like I sounded too eager.

"What are you doing later?"

"Uh, I don't know; Christina is here. We are having a pajama party."

He sent a smiling emoji in reply. "Sounds fun. Can I text you tomorrow?"

"Sure." I thought it was odd he asked, but he was polite that way.

"Enjoy!"

I put the phone back on the table.

"Who was that?"

Not really wanting to tell Christina it was Daniel, because I knew she got that smug look that said, "I told you so." I hedged for a moment.

"Daniel saying thank you for letting him stay over."

"Hmm mmm." She indeed had a smug look on her face.

I laughed, "you are hopeless."

"So are you."

CHAPTER 19

*J*udy

December 10

I always aspired to be one of those people who shopped all year and saved gifts for Christmas. Or at least remembered what people mentioned they liked, so I'd have ideas when the holidays came around. But I wasn't one of those people—and this year, I had the added pressure of buying something for Nick. What do you buy for a man who has everything and can make anything? I needed help, so I called Harper.

"Hello, it's mom."

"Hi mom, are you at the bakery?"

"Of course. Are you at work?"

"Yes, after taking last Friday off, I thought I would come to work."

"That is probably a good idea. Do you have time to go shopping me with me this evening?"

"I do. You haven't started shopping either?" she laughed. "I'll stop by the bakery after work."

"Okay, later."

I went back to cleaning up the kitchen and checking on the items up front.

The weather had been inconvenient, but it didn't hurt business. People, having been cooped up, flocked to the store once the roads were clear, making up for the days I had to stay closed.

I was setting things up for the next morning when I heard the bell on the door ring, signaling Harper's arrival.

"Mom? You here?"

"I'm here," I walked up front, turning off lights as I went.

"How was business today?"

"It was good, steady. So far, not much keeps people away from a delicious muffin and coffee."

Harper leaned in to give me a quick hug. "That's because yours are the best."

"You're biased. Come on, where shall we start with the shopping?"

"I need something for the people at work, and Christina."

"Does that include Daniel?"

"I don't know."

"You should buy him a little something. He is a friend like Christina, right?" I knew he wasn't a friend like Christina. The problem was my daughter was stubborn, and she hadn't realized Daniel was more yet.

"True."

We walked down the sidewalk to a few of the shops.

"Are you buying anything for Nick?" Harper asked.

"I am but, I'm not sure what exactly. The man has made has everything and can make what he doesn't have."

"What about a gift card to his favorite store?"

"He owns his favorite store." I quipped, "besides I hate gift cards. They are so impersonal. I mean, why even bother?"

"Mom,"

"You know what I mean. They say, here I couldn't be bothered, so go buy yourself something."

"Geeze, now that you put it that way."

"You know I'm right."

"I'm beginning to believe so."

We moved on to a funky little shop that had everything from clothes and jewelry to incense and novelties.

"What in the world are we buying in here?"

"I don't know, mom but loosen up. They have a little of everything. You never know what you might find in here." Harper laughed and led the way.

We visited a few more stores and stopped to admire the lights on the tree as we headed back towards the bakery.

"Do you want to stop somewhere for dinner?"

"Thanks mom, but if you don't mind. I'd rather head home."

"No dear, I don't mind. Are you feeling alright?"

"Just tired."

"Okay, well, give me a hug and I'll talk to you tomorrow."

Harper walked towards her apartment, and I headed for the parking lot behind the bakery. My phone buzzed as I was putting the bags in the car.

"Hello?"

"Hey Judy, it's Nick. Did I catch you at a bad time?"

My heart skipped a beat or two the way it always did when I heard Nick's voice. "No, I was trying to put some shopping in the car."

"Do you need any help?"

"No, just some light bags."

"Long day then?"

"Yes, but they all are when you start at four in the morning." I laughed.

"Why don't you let me cook for you tonight?"

I felt flattered and surprised. "You cook?"

"Well, not as well as you but, I do manage to feed myself." He chuckled.

"Of course you do, I'm sorry."

"Judy, it's okay. I was kidding. Why don't you come over and I'll make us both dinner."

"Okay, I've never been to your house. Is it hard to find?"

"Not at all. I'll text you the address. It's in the garden district. Are you familiar?"

"Yes, I've been there a few times."

"Terrific, I'll send the address, but call me if you have problems."

"See you soon." I dashed back inside and grabbed a pie from the fridge to take for dessert.

Again, my heart was racing as I sat behind the wheel waiting for his text. A moment later, the text arrived. It only took twenty minutes to drive to his house. It was stunning. There were small wreaths on each window and a larger wreath on the door. Two spotlights in the front yard illuminated the house, giving it a stately holiday look. Nick met me at the door.

"I'm so glad you found it with no problem."

"Me too, but it was quite simple." I paused at the door, and he gave me a light kiss on the cheek.

"Come in."

I stepped inside and a delicious scent wafted in from the kitchen. "Something smells wonderful."

"Thank you,"

"I brought dessert." I held out the paper bag.

"You didn't have to do that. Thank you."

"I wanted to," I smiled.

After taking my coat and hanging my purse on the hook with it, I followed him to the kitchen.

"Would you like a glass of wine before dinner?"

"That would be lovely."

"Tell you what, what don't you have a seat in here, and relax. I'll bring the wine." He guided me to the sofa in the cozy living room.

"I can't sit in here while you cook."

"I'll join you in a second."

I frowned but sat down, glancing around the room. It didn't have a masculine feel—no wood paneling or wall art of ducks and deer. The walls were a soft gray, with clean lines and dark blue accents. A Christmas tree stood in the corner, decorated with white lights and red and silver ornaments. Fresh greenery lined the mantel, and there were small touches of Christmas throughout the space. On the bookshelf, a few photos caught my eye: one of a couple I assumed were his parents, another of him and a boy who had to be his brother, given the strong resemblance. And then a picture of Nick in uniform with his unit, somewhere overseas.

I was relieved not to see any photos of another woman, which was ridiculous, but I couldn't help it. I would have felt disappointed if there was a photo of him with an ex-girlfriend or wife.

"Here we go." He brought out a tray with wine and cheese. "Dinner is in the oven. It will be a few more minutes."

"This is lovely,"

He grinned and sat down next to me. The wine's allure faded in an instant. My attention shifted to the softness of his flannel shirt and the subtle shadow of stubble on his jaw. Without thinking, I inched a little closer. He handed me the wineglass, and we both leaned back on the sofa. I took a sip, closing my eyes as my muscles began to relax. I hadn't felt this at ease in a long time—maybe ever.

"Hmm, this is wonderful." I breathed.

"Good, I'm glad."

We sat sipping wine and staring at the fire until a timer sounded in the kitchen.

"Wait right here while I check on that."

"Are you sure I can't help?"

"Quite sure."

I inclined my head appreciatively, relieved to have a break from kitchen duties. Plucking a morsel of cheese, I savored the moment. This arrangement could swiftly become a cherished habit. As I drained the last of my wine, Nick made his reappearance.

"Dinner is served." He held out his hand. He escorted me to the dining room table.

"Tonight, we have a fillet of Sole with rosemary, new potatoes, and carrots."

"This looks amazing!"

He held my chair for me and then served each of us. I took a small bite.

"Nick, this is incredible. I think you missed your calling. You should have been a chef."

He laughed a sexy, deep laugh. "No thank you, you all keep long hours."

"True enough." I took another bite.

We talked about how our respective days had been, then the conversation turned to Christmas.

"Do you and Harper spend Christmas together?"

"Yes, some years one of the boys will come into town and it gets messy and loud at my house for about a week. What about you? I noticed the family photos earlier."

"Oh well, my brother died several years ago, my mother shortly afterwards. My father is in a memory care facility. I go see him, but most of the time he doesn't know who I am."

"Oh, I am so sorry. I didn't realize that."

"Don't be sorry. It's life, and it happens."

"I am surprised I didn't know before now."

"Well, it isn't the best topics of conversation." He smiled. "It can drag a conversation down quickly."

"I see your point." I smiled warmly at him. He was such a sweet man; it was hard to remember sometimes that he had been through so much. Most people would be angry or bitter. "Well, then, how about you and I spend Christmas together?" The words flew out of my mouth with no filter at all.

"Are you sure? I don't want to intrude on your family time."

"You're being silly!" I couldn't say what I was thinking, which was that I wanted him under my Christmas tree.

"Thank you, that is very sweet. But I don't want to impose."

"If you're invited, it isn't an intrusion, but there is no pressure." I needed to give him an out. He leaned over to me and gently placed his hand on the back of my neck, cradling it as I looked up at him.

"There is no place I'd rather be for Christmas or any day."

"Oh," I tried to say, but it came out more than a sigh, before he kissed me. God, how this man could kiss.

He broke the kiss and smiled. "You taste so sweet."

I could feel my face blush. I didn't know what to say, so I kissed him this time.

He guided me back to the living room, and we sat on the sofa.

"Judy,"

I looked up into those eyes. I didn't want this night to end.

"Nick," I breathed as if his name was life itself. He ran his finger along my jawline to my lips.

"God, you are so beautiful."

I ducked my eyes; it was hard to hold his gaze amid such a compliment. "You're so handsome," I said, meeting his gaze again and cradling his face with both my hands.

"Stay with me tonight." He nuzzled my neck. "I didn't mean to put you on the spot, it was just that. I don't want this night to end."

"Me neither." I said as he kissed my throat, then my mouth. I never wanted this night to end.

He studied my face, silently questioning if I wanted to stay. I nodded.

"Yeah?" He whispered.

I bit my lower lip, "Yeah." In one fluid motion, he picked me up and carried me upstairs to his room. My heart raced, and I trembled. I reminded myself that I was a grown woman with children and if I wanted to spend the night with a man I cared deeply for, then that is what I was going to do.

CHAPTER 20

Harper

I finished most of my Christmas shopping, but I was still undecided about a gift for Daniel. Was it all too much, too soon? I entertained the thought of starting a new career with online dating advice, with the first rule being: *never start a new relationship right before the holidays*—it adds way too much pressure. But I was sure someone had done that before. Daniel and I weren't even dating, something I'd told Christina multiple times, but I'd feel terrible if he bought me something and I had nothing for him. Then there was the issue of what to get him. Nothing too impersonal, like a gift card—that wasn't the way to go—but I didn't want anything too personal either. I considered ghosting him for a while, but that wasn't who I was, and it was a terrible thing to do to anyone.

I laid in bed with Yeti curled up next to me and a book open in my lap, my mind drifting off to a fantasy world where Daniel replaced the main character in the book. Maybe I should ask him how he felt about a Christmas present. Who knows, maybe he was struggling with the same question. My eyes were getting heavy, and I would have to wait to solve this problem tomorrow. Maybe divine inspiration would come to me in a dream.

The alarm went off way too early, and it was so tempting to stay under the covers and snuggle with Yeti, but I was only putting off the inevitable. I clicked on the weather as I got ready for work. It was warm enough for the ice to have melted.

I planned to schedule a meeting for the remaining holiday events going on until the new year. I checked calendars of the group for the week and then sent out a meeting invitation. By the end of the day, I had gotten a response to the meeting request from everyone but Daniel, so I thought I would stop by his office on the way out this evening. I stopped by his office around five, but he wasn't there. I was surprised by how disappointed I felt.

Yeti and I spent a quiet evening at home and by noon the next day, I still hadn't heard from Daniel. I was getting worried. I realize it was irrational. Maybe he had taken a few days off. He was under no obligation to tell me his plans. But if I was honest, I was bouncing between hurt that he hadn't confided in his plans and panic that he was sick or had had a car accident and was in a hospital in a coma or something.

I took a deep breath and tried to stop my mind from going to crazy places.

When five o'clock came and I still hadn't heard from him, I texted him to check on him. By eight that evening, I still hadn't heard from him. I was getting worried now. It had been two days now, so I called my mother.

"Hello?"

"Mom, it's me."

"Harper, what's wrong?"

"Why do you think something is wrong?"

"I can hear it in your voice."

"Well, since you asked, I wondered if Nick has heard from Daniel in the past forty-eight hours. He hasn't been at work for two days and he didn't response to a text I sent earlier today."

"Oh, I'm sure he is fine. He probably took a couple of days off."

"Yeah, I keep telling myself that."

"If it makes you feel better, I can ask Nick."

I hated I was about to say yes, but I had to know he was okay. I imagine my mother's face giving me that 'I knew it' look.

"If you wouldn't mind."

"Okay dear. Can I call you back?"

I hung up and sunk onto the sofa in a deep funk, hoping that Daniel was okay and hating the fact that I did care for him more than I wanted. Only yesterday I had been ready to pull away from him, to avoid this situation, of getting invested, only to have my heart broken.

I sat, biting my thumbnail, waiting anxiously for my mother to call me back. Five, ten, fifteen minutes passed with no word. I checked my phone again to make sure the battery wasn't dead, then carried it with me to the kitchen as I fixed a cup of tea. What was taking so long? If everything were fine, she would've called right back. My tension mounted with each passing minute.

Yeti wandered into the kitchen, circling his food bowl. I stooped to pet him and added a few crunchies. This was ridiculous—I was overreacting. Daniel and I were barely friends. Sure, we'd been hanging out a lot lately, and he'd crashed on my sofa twice, but there was no romance, no promises. He didn't owe me any explanations. So, what if he ghosted me? Why should I care? I didn't even want a relationship.

My emotions spiraled, and frustration boiled over. I stomped back into the living room, flopped down on the sofa, and grabbed my phone to call my mom—ready to tell her to forget about it, to apologize for bothering her and Nick with my irrational panic.

My phone rang before I could punch in her number.

"Hello?"

"Hi, it's Daniel."

My heart skipped, and a wave of relief washed over me.

"Hey, how are you?" I said instead of 'are you alright?' and 'where have you been?'

"Sorry for the delay in responding to your text earlier, but I'm fine. I had to fly down to Florida at the last minute."

"Florida?"

"My mom lives in a retirement village down here. She fell and broke her hip."

"Oh my gosh, will she be okay?"

"Yeah, she's going to be fine. They are going to keep her for a couple of days. I'm still working how where we go from here."

"Is there anything I can do to help?"

He chuckled softly. "I don't think so."

"How did she fall?"

"She was roller blading with some friends."

I couldn't help it. I laughed. "She was doing what?"

"Yeah, roller blading. I love she is young at heart, but her body isn't as young as her spirit, so things like this happen."

"What about Malin? Do you need me to feed her or anything?"

"No, my neighbor has that under control." I heard some noise in the background. "Sorry I gotta run. I'll try to text you an update later."

"Okay, well, let me know if you think of something I can do to help."

"Thanks, I will. Gotta run. Bye."

And he was gone. I stared at the phone for several minutes, the silence in my apartment growing louder with each passing second. I glanced down at Yeti. "Well, say something," I muttered. He flicked his fluffy tail and strolled away. Of course, any other time he'd be demanding attention.

I felt utterly helpless. All I wanted was to hop on a plane and fly down to Florida to help Daniel. Only two problems with that: flying there might send the wrong message, and what could I really do? And I didn't even know what city he was in.

Putting on some Christmas music, I sat down at the table and began working on my Christmas cards. I should have sent them out weeks ago. An hour later, I had them all signed, addressed and stamped. I'd put them in the mail in the morning. Then I pulled out my Christmas checklist that I had been neglecting, determined to update it and focus on any unfinished items. As I flipped through my appointment book for the rest of the week, I found a note I had written to myself to set new goals for the new year.

Taking a step back, I reflected on the past year. I picked up Yeti and set him in my lap while I thought about it. What had I done in the past year that I enjoyed? What had I done that I didn't enjoy? I pulled out a clean sheet of paper, making two columns and listing things in each category. When I was done, I determined what I needed in the new year was a new job.

Everything stressful in my life over the past year seemed tied to my job. While I knew no job would ever be stress free, it had become obvious—I needed a change. The realization hit me hard. I was tired of event planning. I needed something different, but that was the real challenge. What would I do next? With less than a month left in the year, the pressure was on to figure it out. I didn't expect to have a new job by January 1st, but I needed a plan, a clear sense of what I wanted next.

Leaning back, I allowed myself a moment of satisfaction. Despite everything left to tackle in December, I had accomplished more than I realized. Thanksgiving felt like it had been just last week, and the month was flying by. I was gradually regaining control.

I took a deep breath and called my mom back.

"Hi mom, it's me."

"Hi sweetie, did you hear from Daniel?"

"What? Oh yeah, he's fine. He's mom broke her hip roller blading, and he rushed to be with her."

"Sounds like she and I could be friends."

"She lives in Florida."

"Too bad."

"Mom, you don't have time for roller blading."

"Sad, but true."

"The reason I am calling is I finished going over my calendar for the rest of the year and I wanted to see what you need help with for Christmas dinner."

"Oh, that reminds me. Tommy called to confirm they are coming for Christmas, so we will have four more people to feed." My mom announced.

"Wow, that's great. But that puts a little more pressure on the dinner. Do we need another turkey?" I asked.

"No, I'm thinking of just adding a roast. Give everyone options."

I nodded to myself. "Sounds good. Okay, why don't I make the roast then? That will be one less thing you have to worry about."

"Thanks, yes, that would be helpful, sweetie."

"Not to change the subject, but have you sent your cards out yet?"

" I just finished them up and they are going out in the morning."

"Wanna come over tomorrow and help me with mine?"

"Absolutely, and then we can go over the menu for Christmas dinner and see what we can make ahead of time."

"Sounds like a plan. Are you going to invite Daniel?"

"I hadn't given it much thought."

"I'm surprised."

"Why?"

"A couple of hours ago you were in panic mode because you were worried about him, not you're saying you haven't thought about inviting him to Christmas dinner?"

"Well, just because I won't want him to be injured in a car accident doesn't mean I am going to invite him to dinner."

"Yes, but you have been spending a lot of time together."

"True," I sighed. Not wanting to have this conversation, I sighed and said, "I will ask him, but don't be disappointed if he stays in Florida to be with his mother during the holidays, mom."

"Oh, I won't be disappointed. I hope you're not."

"I'm too busy to worry about it. Now let's talk menu. I know we have more people this year, but that means we need a bigger turkey."

"True, and I already have one. I ordered one from one of my suppliers."

"Okay, great. Which side dishes do you want me to make?"

We talked for another hour while I made notes about the Christmas dinner menu. By the time I went to bed, I was feeling much better about life for the next few weeks.

CHAPTER 21

❄

*H*arper

December 22nd

The days leading up to Christmas had flown by, filled with end-of-year reports, last-minute grant applications, and planning for spring events. I'd seen Daniel a couple of times in meetings, but neither of us had the time to talk. I asked about his mother, and we promised to have dinner, but it never happened. To me, that was a sign—I was right. This wasn't the time for a relationship. Relief washed over me, though a hint of disappointment lingered.

I didn't have time to dwell on Daniel. Today was the last day of work before Christmas. I had taken off at noon and was on my way to Norfolk to pick my brother and his family at the airport. Traffic was going to be heavy with holiday travelers and the never-ending construction on Interstate 64.

As I merged into traffic approaching the bridge tunnel, everything slowed down. I took a deep breath, trying not to stress. I checked my brother's flight status—still on time and I had an hour to get there. Hopefully, traffic would speed up once we got through the construction zone. So much for the widening project that was supposed to fix this mess.

As we creeped and crawled, I turned up the Christmas music. If I was late, my brother would just have to wait. He was a frequent traveler for his job, so I was sure he was used to traveling delays. Finally, I made it to Norfolk and drove as quickly as the law would allow to the airport. I sent my brother a text, and he assured me they would wait outside. I inched along until I finally spotted them waving on the curb, and I pulled up to load everyone up in my car.

"Tommy!" I cried as I hugged my brother. I had two brothers; Tommy was the youngest. He had always been my nemesis while growing until he and Eddie went off to college. Tommy was married to Ellen and had two beautiful boys, Josh, and Eli.

"Hey sis! How are you?"

"I'm great." I hugged my sister-in-law. "Ellen, you look beautiful."

"So good to see you. Thank you so much for picking us up."

"Of course! And do I get a hug from my two favorite nephews?" I turned to Eli and Josh.

"Aunt Harper!" They both hugged me around the waist.

"You guys are getting so tall!" Josh was ten and Eli was eight. They had grown a foot since the last time I had seen them.

"Grandma is going to be so excited to see you!" I ruffled their hair. "Come on, let's get in the car where it's warm."

With everyone tucked into the car, we headed back across the water. I put on Christmas music and the boys sang all the way back to the mom's house. Being around kids for extended periods was something I wasn't used to. I had a feeling this was going to be a long night.

Mom sent a text to make sure I found Tommy and family. I handed my phone to Tommy and had him respond to mom, while I concentrated on the road.

The trip back was almost as long as the trip over there because of an accident in the tunnel, reminding me yet again why I rarely come to the south side.

When we pulled into the driveway, and Mom was waiting at the door.

"Wow!" the boys exclaimed, seeing all the Christmas lights and decorations on the house.

I laughed, "Wait 'til you see the inside."

Tommy looked over at me. "Are you serious?"

"She went all out when she found out you all were coming for Christmas. She wants everything to be perfect."

"She doesn't need to do all of this," Ellen protested.

"Try telling her that." I laughed, opening the car door. The boys were already out of the car and racing towards the house.

Ellen looked over the top of the car at me. "No, thanks."

"Smart woman," Tommy said, lifting their luggage out of the trunk.

I noticed Nick's truck wasn't here, and I wondered when mom would tell Tommy she had a boyfriend. Hopefully, before Nick showed up for Christmas dinner.

I followed the little family inside and watched as my mother's face lit up with her grandson's attention. She hugged Tommy and Ellen and then returned her attention back to Josh and Eli.

"How was your trip?" She asked as they peeled off their coats.

"It was okay. We played video games until the plan landed."

"Oh, okay." She smiled. "Are you hungry?"

"Judy, they ate before we got on the plane." Ellen explained.

"What did you have?" She looked at the boys.

I knew where this was going. I whispered to Tommy, "Wait for it."

"We had burgers."

"Burgers?" My mom put her hands on her hips. "Just burgers?"

"Yes, ma'am." Eli said.

"Well, that doesn't sound festive."

Josh and Eli looked at one another, confused. "I think you two need Christmas cookies and milk."

"Yea!" they both shouted, then looked over at Ellen.

"Go ahead."

"Come with me." Mom ushered the boys to the kitchen.

Tommy looked at me and then Ellen, "well they are going to be up all night."

Ellen nodded. "They were too excited to sleep, anyway."

"Well come one, we might as well partake." I said, heading to the kitchen.

Two different conversations filled the room, with my mother absorbed in everything her grandsons were telling her. Tommy, Ellen, and I then retreated to the living room with wine and beer after sampling mom's cookies.

"Mom tells me you are dating someone?" Tommy asked.

I looked at him like he was insane. "What? No!"

Ellen looked at me concerned, "You're not?"

"No, I don't have time for that."

"So, you weren't hanging out with some guy from work?"

I bristled. "If she was referring to Daniel, we work

together and hang out together once in a while, but I've barely seen him in weeks."

"Do I need to have a talk with him about how he treats my sister?" Tommy joked.

"You have never cared one way or another who I dated. Eddie was the one that scared away all my boyfriends." I argued.

Ellen sipped her wine. She was used to our sibling rivalry. I wished my brothers had been a little younger. They moved away and got married. I didn't see my sister in laws often, but Ellen was my favorite, probably because she was closer to my age. Finally, the boys went to bed and while my mother had Tommy to herself, Ellen and I sat drinking cocoa.

"So, tell me about this guy you work with. Is he at least good looking?" Ellen asked.

I hesitated, not wanting to rehash the whole Daniel thing.

"Yes, he is quite handsome."

"How did you meet? I mean, do you work in the same department?"

"No, he works in the budget office, and we are often on the same committees for events since he holds the purse strings."

Ellen leaned back in her chair. "Ut-oh, I sense trouble."

"We didn't always get along and, to be honest, that was mostly my fault. I painted him as a scrooge when he was just doing his job."

"What made you change your mind?"

"Well, we had an early snowstorm, and I lost power at my apartment for a few days. He and I ran into each other, and he sort of rescued me."

"How so?"

"I was out looking for coffee. He was out jogging. His house had power, so he invited me back to his place to have coffee and warm up."

"That was nice of him." Her voice remained neutral.

"It was. He lives in this beautiful Victorian. He restored it himself and he loves Christmas movies, so we sat watching one until I fell asleep on his sofa."

Ellen giggled, "Awkward."

"No kidding, then he gave me a ride over here so that I could stay with mom until power was restored."

"And then what?"

"Uh well we went to lunch a few times and," I smiled at the memory, "There was still a lot of snow on the ground, and we went out to the old fort, and we found a mama cat and a kitten nearly frozen to death and we scooped them up and took them to the emergency vet. He adopted the momma cat, and I adopted the kitten."

"Now, he rescues animals too?"

"Yeah." I shrugged.

Ellen was playing it cool. "So, have you seen much of him since then?"

"Well, there was this one day when we had an ice storm and the streets were frozen when we came out of work so, since I live within walking distance, I offered him to stay over at my place until the streets became safe, you know, sort of returning the favor."

"Totally get it." She nodded; this is why she was my favorite.

"I haven't seen much of him since then. His mother lives in Florida and she fell, so he went down to take care of her."

"What you are telling me is that this guy is handsome, rescues damsels in distress, kittens in the snow, and takes care of old ladies?"

"When you say it like that…."

"You're right to avoid him. I mean, no one is that perfect and the ones that are serial killers."

I looked at her, waiting for the punchline.

"Seriously, he restored a creepy old Victorian, that screams of secret passageways to a basement where he keeps his victims. You're lucky to be alive."

I wasn't sure if she was serious or not. It's the kind of thing that would be an excellent episode for a true crime show. For a second, I wondered if she might be right. An accountant was the perfect cover story. No one would think a nerdy accountant would hide a woman in his basement.

Ellen abruptly burst out laughing. I wasn't sure if I wanted to laugh or be mad at her. She laughed so hard she snorted.

"I'm sorry," she said when she got enough air. "The look on your face was priceless."

I chuckled, not quite as amused as Ellen. I could see why she and Tommy got along so well.

"Oh, sweetie, I was totally joking. You don't really believe this guy would harm anyone."

"No, I don't." I said honestly. "But no one is perfect. What's his flaw? He must have one."

"His flaw is that he hasn't realized how amazing you are yet, and he hasn't snatched you up."

"Yeah, well, I'm not sure that would do him any good."

"What do you mean?"

"I'm not into relationships. They never last and end badly."

Ellen got serious. "Not all of them."

I didn't want to argue with her and point out the obvious. "Yeah, well, the ones I've seen have imploded."

"Tommy and I have been married twelve years, and we are still in love. That doesn't mean we don't have spats from time to time. But we're solid."

I resisted the urge to say, 'so far'. Tommy was also a victim of my father's abandonment, and I wondered which of the boys would follow in his footsteps. But they both seem to have very stable lives.

"I don't know." I shook my head. "It is something I've never planned on, you know?"

"So, you don't want to get married?"

"No offense to you and Tommy, but no. I don't want to experience what mom experienced with Dad."

Ellen's features softened. "Oh honey, you can't let one man out of millions prevent you from being happy. It is like he is still hurting you more than when he was alive."

I stared at her. I hadn't thought of it that way and she had a point. But it was going to take some reprogramming on my part. She leaned over and put an arm around my shoulder.

"Listen, I'm not saying this guy Daniel is the one, but I believe the one is out there and you shouldn't let something that happened thirty years ago rob you of your future today."

A hot tear rolled down my cheek. She was right, and I felt like an idiot. "You're right. I've been letting him hurt me repeatedly."

Exhausted, I went to bed, Ellen's words echoing in my head as I drifted off to sleep.

CHAPTER 22

❄

Harper

December 23rd

The sounds of Josh and Eli laughing and running down the stairs greeted me as I woke up. I needed coffee.

I dressed and padded downstairs in search of a caffeine fix. I was sure my mother had already left for the bakery; this was a busy time of year for her.

"Morning, Aunt Harper!" Eli shouted.

Ug, "Morning Eli."

"Are you going to hang out with us today?"

"Sure bud, let me get a cup of coffee first and then we can plan our day, okay?"

"Okay." He looked disappointed.

Ellen walked into the kitchen. "Eli, go finish your breakfast and don't bother Harper until she has had a chance to wake up."

"Okay mom." He trudged off.

"Sorry about that." Ellen gave me a sympathetic smile.

"It's okay. He's excited. I wish I could be that eager first thing in the morning."

She laughed, "Me, too. I'm exhausted by ten on the weekends."

I took a couple of restorative sips of coffee. I closed my eyes and waited for it to work its magic.

"Ah, there, that is better." I smiled at Ellen. "What is the plan for the day?"

"I was hoping to take them to see your Christmas tree your mom told us about and some ice skating."

"Sounds good. I need to run home and change and feed my cat. I'll meet you there around eleven?"

"Thanks Harper, I appreciate it."

"Oh, did mom leave you, her car?"

"She did. Tommy took her to work this morning. I told her we could get a rental, but she insisted."

"That's mom for you." I put the lid on my travel cup and gathered up my things and drove home. Yeti wasn't talking to me because he had to sleep alone the night before despite having plenty of crunchies and fresh water. He got over his anger long enough to come and get some pate.

I showered and changed into something more fitting for an afternoon with my two nephews. Just as I was about to head out to meet them at the skating rink, my phone buzzed with a text. To my surprise, it was from Daniel.

"Hey, sorry, I haven't been around lately. Do you have time for lunch?"

I stared at the phone, debating whether to respond. Ellen's words from the night before still echoed in my mind. After a moment, I replied.

"I'm spending the day with my nephews. You're welcome to join us. We are going to go ice skating."

"I don't want to infringe on family time," he replied.

If you're invited, you're not infringing. I pocketed the phone and left. I had made an offer, and it was up to him whether he joined us or not.

Tommy, Ellen, and the boys already had their skates on when I got to the rink.

"Aunt Harper, are you going to skate?" Eli called out.

"I'll watch for a minute. You go ahead; I'll catch up."

"Come on Eli, dad says Aunt Harper can't skate, anyway." Josh laughed.

I knew Tommy had put him up to saying that.

"Oh, really?"

Tommy laughed as he joined the boys on the ice.

"Don't listen to them," Ellen said. "You don't have to skate at all."

"I'll be there in a minute."

I glanced around hoping to see Daniel, disappointed I walked over to rent a pair of skates.

"That will be seven dollars." The attendant smiled.

I felt a hand on my arm. "I'll need a pair as well, size twelve." Daniel handed the attendant cash over and winked at me as we accepted our skates.

"Hey," I said breathless, my heart was racing, and I felt like I couldn't breathe.

He turned to me, "Hey."

I caught Ellen looking at us from across the rink and smiling before she pulled on Tommy's sleeve.

Turning back to Daniel, "Thanks for coming."

"You're welcome. I'm sorry I've been out of touch lately. I know it must seem like I ghosted you after you let me stay over."

"No, not at all. You have a lot going on right now. How is

your mom?"

He chuckled. "She'll be fine. She needs to rest and take it easy, and she'll have physical therapy for a while, but she'll be okay."

"Are you going back down to spend Christmas with her?"

"No, she had other plans for Christmas."

"Really?" I was surprised. What mother doesn't want to spend Christmas with her son?

"She and some of her girlfriends already had something planned, and she intended to go through with it, so I came home."

"Are you okay with that?"

"That she had other plans? Oh yeah, that isn't unusual since she moved to Florida. She has more of a social life than I do. I wanted to make sure she was okay and got everything set up for her. She knows I'll be there in a matter of hours if she needs me."

I couldn't imagine leaving my mom at Christmas with a broken hip, but it sounded like it wasn't Daniel's first choice, either.

Josh and Eli skated over before I could ask any more questions. "Aunt Harper, you can skate?" Josh sounded surprised.

"I can, and you shouldn't believe everything your dad tells you about me."

He looked over at Tommy, who was laughing. "She couldn't skate when she was a kid."

"Don't wiggle your way out of it."

Eli skated up to Daniel, "Hi, I'm Eli."

"Hi Eli, I'm Daniel, a friend of Harpers."

"Are you her boyfriend?"

"Eli!" Ellen admonished.

Daniel laughed amiably. "No, we are just friends and co-workers."

Even in the cold, I could feel my cheeks blush. Ellen cocked an eyebrow at me. "I'm freezing. Come on boys, let's go get hot chocolate." She ushered the boys away.

Daniel turned to skate backwards, "I'm sorry I didn't properly introduce you to my brother and his wife."

"It's okay. I'll meet them later." He took my hands so I could keep up with him. I skated well enough to stay upright, but I was not graceful, and Daniel was, of course, terrific at ice skating.

"You sure I'm not imposing on family time? I know it has been a while since you have seen your brother."

"Not at all, and they are mostly here to see my mom."

"Where is she?"

"Today is the last day the bakery will be open until after Christmas, so she is there getting out last-minute orders for Christmas rolls and pies."

"She works so hard."

"I know, she has help, but I wish she would let them run the bakery for a day so she could relax for a change.

"Now I know where you get it from."

We were skating towards Tommy and the kids. "You work too hard."

"Look who is talking!" I laughed.

"Don't make this about me." He scolded as we reached Tommy.

We stepped off the ice and sat down.

My brother picked that moment to introduce himself.

"Hi, I'm Tommy. Harper's brother."

"Daniel, nice to meet you."

As they shook hands, I directed a glare at Tommy, hoping it was interpreted as a death stare.

"This is Josh and Eli, and my wife Ellen."

The two boys waved and gawked. Ellen reached out a hand, "Hello I'm so glad you could join us."

Daniel smiled. It was hard to resist Ellen. She was so sweet and charming. I was glad she was married to my brother so I wouldn't have to scratch her eyes out over smiling like that at Daniel.

"Come on kids, let Daniel and Harper take off their skates, then we can go see grandma at the bakery."

"Hooray!" the boys jumped up and down.

Tommy wrangled them over to return everyone's skates. I gave Daniel an apologetic look. "Are you sure you are up for this?"

"It will be fun!" He gave me an adventurous smile.

"Okay, don't say I didn't warn you." I shook my head, and we all headed for mom's bakery.

"Now listen," I turned to caution the boys, "This is a busy day for grandma at work so she might not spend as much time with us as we would like, okay?"

Josh and Eli nodded. Ellen looked worried. "Should we not go in?"

"Mom would kill us all if we didn't bring the boys by. It might be a little crazy in there today. People picking up last-minute rolls and desserts."

Tommy opened the door, and we all piled inside. As soon as she saw Josh and Eli, mom squealed. "My babies!" She ran around to hug them.

I looked around. There were plenty of tables available and only a small line for pickups. "Ellen, let's pull together a couple of tables over here in the corner."

Daniel and Tommy jumped in to help. I shed my coat. "Mom, do you need help behind the counter so you can spend time with the boys?"

"Do you mind? Just a few minutes?"

"I don't mind," I said, turning to Daniel. "I'll be back in a few minutes."

"Take your time. I'm going to hang out with your brother," he replied.

Tommy shot me an evil grin, and I gave him a warning look, but there was no time to argue.

I quickly got to work behind the counter, helping the other employees. Since I often helped Mom out, I was more like a part-time employee at this point. I knew the system and how to use the register, so I blended into the team easily, picking up tasks without missing a beat.

We had the line down in a matter of minutes while mom fed everyone cookies and hot cocoa.

After we had warmed up and the boys were on a sugar high, we went back out into the cold for the boys to get a behind-the-scenes tour of the Christmas lights and the tree. The sky was getting dark early, with clouds rolling in. I looked up at the sky.

"Those look like snow clouds." I said to no one in particular.

Daniel and Tommy looked up.

"You could be right," Daniel said. "We've had some unseasonably cold weather already this year."

"Snow here? For Christmas?" Tommy scoffed.

"I get it isn't Delaware," I sniped, "But, we've had snow once already and an ice storm, so it is possible."

"Are we going to get snow, Aunt Harper?"

"It looks like it to me, but I was probably your age the last time we had snow for Christmas."

"Wow." Eli said in amazement.

Josh was beyond excited. "I hope we get snow, and we get to stay at grandma's house longer!"

"Yeah!" Eli shouted.

"God, I hope not. They will drive your mother crazy." Ellen whispered.

"Oh, she survived Tommy and Eddie. She can handle Josh and Eli."

"What about you?" Ellen laughed.

"I'll lock myself in my apartment with my cat and be the spinster in training that I am."

We both laughed. Daniel gave me an odd look but didn't comment.

Finally, Tommy and Ellen took mom and the boy's home. Daniel and I walked towards my apartment.

"Do you want to stop for dinner?" he asked.

"I don't know. I'm not that hungry, but soup would be wonderful."

"What kind?"

"I'm craving hot and sour soup."

Daniel grinned, "let's go back to your place and relax and I know the perfect place we can order takeout."

"That sounds perfect."

He reached over and took my hand; I was surprised, but I didn't pull back.

"There is one condition, though," I said, keeping eyes straight ahead.

"Oh?"

"We have to watch a Christmas movie."

"That goes without saying." He laughed.

I turned to look at him. He was serious. He was too good to be true. Ellen's words echoed in my mind.

As if he could read my thoughts, Daniel looked at me. "What was that earlier about you being a spinster?"

"Oh, Ellen, has this crazy idea that I need to open myself up to the possibility of romance more."

"Do you?"

I realized I had probably said too much and blushed. "Do I what?"

"Close yourself away from romance?"

"Hmm, that is a loaded question."

"It wasn't meant to be."

"Well, I. I've never thought about long-term relationships based on my parents' experience."

He looked at me, surprised.

"What?"

He stopped in front of my building and looked at me. "You mean you watch all these romantic Christmas movies but never thought about the same type of relationship for yourself?"

"Yeah, I know I'm weird." I chuckled, trying to cover up my embarrassment.

"I don't think you're weird, well, at least not for that reason."

I looked at him, and he smiled, sending us both into fits of laugher.

"Good to know." I opened the door to my apartment, and the roar of a tiny hungry kitty greeted us.

CHAPTER 23

✻

*N*ick

December 24th

The workshop behind Jansen's hardware was quieter than usual. The store was closed so employees could be with their families. A nearly finished wooden train sat in front of me, its wheels waiting to be attached. Normally, I'd have Daniel here helping me—he loved putting the finishing touches on these toys for the kids at the Children's Hospital. But Daniel was busy with Harper, so I used that as a chance to ask Judy to come with me to the hospital.

Her laugh, as warm as fresh-baked bread, always made me feel at ease. She had a way of understanding things—like the magic in something as simple as a hand-carved toy. It was a long shot, but I couldn't think of anyone better to help me finish these toys and deliver them.

I sighed, glancing at the small pile of toys I'd completed on my own: wooden rocking horses, cars, and trains, all polished to a soft sheen. Santa's deadline was looming, and I needed help.

I picked up my phone, my fingers hesitating over her number. Asking her to help wasn't the hard part—it was telling her the truth about why these toys mattered so much. The kids at the hospital knew Santa delivered handmade toys every year. They couldn't tell it was me beneath the white beard.

With a sigh, I dialed her number. Her voice was a balm to my soul.

"Nick? Merry Christmas Eve," Judy said, and I could hear the smile in her voice.

"Hey Judy," I said, trying to keep my tone casual, "Merry Christmas Eve. Listen, I was wondering if you could do me a favor?"

"Of course," she replied. "What's going on?"

"I need a little help this evening," I said, pausing for a moment. "Daniel's busy, and I've got some toys that need to be delivered to the Children's Hospital. I was hoping you might come along with me."

There was a beat of silence, and I could imagine her standing there, her apron dusted with flour, thinking it over.

"Toys for the Children's Hospital?" she repeated softly.

"Yeah," I said, rubbing a hand across the back of my neck. "Every year, I make toys for the kids. It's kind of a tradition … something I've been doing for years."

Her voice softened even more, and I could hear the warmth in it. "I had no idea. Nick, that's wonderful. I'd love to help."

Relief flooded through me. "Great. I'll pick you up in an hour, then."

As I hung up, I felt a strange mix of anticipation and

nerves. Tonight wasn't just about delivering toys—it was about letting Judy see a part of myself I rarely shared with anyone.

An hour later, I pulled up in Judy's driveway. She met me at the door. I thought it was a little out of character, but I didn't complain. I knew she had her family there, and I thought perhaps she needed a break.

"Hey," she greeted me with a smile. "Ready to play Santa?"

I chuckled, but didn't meet her eyes. "Yeah, something like that."

As we drove to the hospital, the snow fell steadily, covering the streets in a soft white blanket. I was quiet, more focused than usual. In my mind, I kept repeating the words I wanted to say to her. I worried she would think I was silly for playing Santa for the kids.

When we pulled up to the Children's hospital, I finally spoke. "There's something I should tell you before we go inside."

"What is it?"

"I've been delivering these toys to the hospital for about fifteen years now. I don't just make them, Judy—I play Santa. The kids don't know it's me, but every Christmas Eve, I put on the suit, and I hand them the toys." I studied her face, looking for signs she would laugh or think it ridiculous.

"Nick ... that's amazing. Why didn't you tell me?"

I shrugged, looking out at the snow-covered hospital entrance. "I never wanted it to be about me. It's about the kids—their smiles, their joy. But tonight ... I guess I wanted you to know. Plus, I thought you might think I was silly for playing dress up."

Judy took my hand in hers. "I'm honored that you told me. Really. And I'd love to help you deliver the toys tonight. You're doing something incredible, Nick."

He looked at me then, his eyes softening. "Thanks, Judy."

Together, we unloaded the toys from the truck and carried them inside, where the staff welcomed us with warm smiles.

I could feel Judy watching as I greeted each child with a gentle smile, handing out the handmade toys one by one. The kids' faces lit up with joy as they opened their presents, and seeing the joy and magic in their tiny faces warmed my heart.

When the last toy had been given out, and out of sight of the children, I pulled off the Santa hat, running my hand through my hair. I met Judy's eyes from across the room. I knew it was the right thing to do to bring her with me tonight. And I knew I was right about my decision to propose to her.

"Ready to head out?" I asked.

As we stepped out into the chilly night, I knew something had shifted between us.

"Nick," Judy said softly as we reached the truck, "thank you for letting me be a part of this."

"Thank you for being here."

We held hands as I drove her back to the central district.

"Nick, can you show me your workshop before you take me back home?"

I glanced over at her, smiling. "Absolutely."

I navigated the streets to the hardware store; I parked around back and took her to the workshop entrance.

I flicked on the lights, and she let out a small gasp. "You have everything in here. I would have never guessed this was back here behind the store!"

She walked around, marveling at the tools. She ran her hand along the workbench.

She stood in the middle of the room. "You're full of surprises, Nick Tanner." She smiled.

I joined her, taking both of her hands. "So, you don't think it is ridiculous. I come back here and play Santa by making toys for the kids?"

"I think it is the most beautiful thing I've ever heard of!" She reached up and touched my cheek. I closed my eyes. It felt so right to have her here with me.

"Next year, I'll bake them some cookies to take along."

"Next year?" I asked, surprised.

"Oh, I'm sorry. I didn't mean to overstep." She blushed.

"No! I'd love for you to come with me. I think the kids would love a treat along with their toy."

"I could be your elf." She laughed.

I walked over to the workbench and removed the ring box I had stored there while I was working and rejoined Judy in the center of the room.

"I was going to do this tomorrow in front of your family, but this is more appropriate."

She looked at me questioningly.

"I think you'd make a better Mrs. Claus." I smiled.

"What?" her voice a whisper.

I opened the box and got down on one knee. "Judy, will you marry me?"

I could tell she was shocked, and I held my breath for what seemed like an eternity.

"Yes."

I thought I had misheard her. "Yes?"

She began to cry, "Yes."

I slipped the ring on her finger and then picked her up and swung her around. "I love you, Judy."

"I love you, Nick!"

I held her for a minute before asking. "Should we go tell Harper?"

"No. Let's have this all to ourselves for just a little bit longer."

"Dinner?" I offered.

"Yes."

"Perfect. I know just the spot. We can share it with the world later."

CHAPTER 24

❄

*J*udy

Christmas Day

From an early age, I never outgrew the habit of waking up early on Christmas morning, always with a little excitement in my stomach. This Christmas morning was even more special and the butterflies in my stomach were on high alert. I gazed down at my engagement ring, enjoying the feeling of excitement, love, and that it was something special just between Nick and me for a few more minutes. The house was still quiet as I listened for any sounds from downstairs. I put on my comfy sweats and headed to the living room, where I turned on all the Christmas lights, including the ones on the tree. Taking a few moments to appreciate the decorations—the stockings, the garland, and especially the tree—each one stirred fond memories that warmed my heart. I also smiled at the thought of new Christmas memories with Nick. I slipped the ring off and placed it carefully in the box. We had agreed to tell the family together this evening at dinner.

The coffee machine beeped, and I added a dash of cinnamon to my cup. I was tempted to turn on the TV. Usually, I had a few peaceful hours to myself on Christmas morning, watching my favorite movie before the day descended into chaos—that had been my personal tradition. But this year was anything but normal. The house was packed with people, and I couldn't have been happier. I knew it wouldn't be long before the boys came barreling downstairs to see what Santa had left.

Popping some cinnamon rolls into the oven, I sipped my coffee, enjoying the brief moment of peace before the holiday excitement began.

I had barely downed half a cup of coffee before I heard footsteps bounding down the stairs and the sound of excited voices as the boys rushed into the den to find the presents under the tree.

"Wow, look at that!" Josh exclaimed.

"Whoa!"

"Good morning." I said from the doorway.

"Grandma!" They both rushed over and hugged me. "Did you see?"

"I did," I smiled at them. "Don't you think you should wait for your parents to come down before you start playing with all the cool stuff under the tree?"

"Aww," they collectively groaned.

Josh brightened, "What about the presents that aren't wrapped, those are from Santa and so mom and dad won't miss us opening those."

I heard movement upstairs, and I was certain it was Tommy and Ellen. "Okay, but only the Santa gifts."

"Hooray!" They rushed to the tree, dropping to their knees.

A moment later, Ellen joined me in the kitchen. I handed her a cup of coffee. "Thank you," she smiled and headed for the den.

"Mom! Come look!" Eli shouted.

"Boys, boys, keep it down. Your aunt Harper might still be sleeping."

"No such luck." Harper said, arriving in the kitchen in flannel pajamas and slippers. Not wanting to miss any of the excitement on Christmas morning, Harper had stayed the night.

Eli rushed over and grabbed her hand, pulling her to the tree. "Look Aunt Harper, we got new skates!"

"Wow, you boys will have to try them out later."

"Will you come with us?"

"Sure, if you let me drink my coffee first."

The boys looked disappointed for only for a moment. They quickly forgot about Harper as they made plans to go ice skating later.

Tommy was the last to arrive.

"Welcome to Christmas chaos." I laughed, handing him a cup of coffee.

Tommy grabbed coffee and joined the boys in the den.

Finally, the adults sat down to exchange gifts.

Everyone had cinnamon buns to hold them over. The boys were eager to try out their skates, so Ellen and Tommy took them to the outdoor ice rink.

"Aunt Harper, you're coming too, right?"

"You go ahead, I'll meet you there."

Ellen ushered the boys out the door. "Your aunt Harper can't spend every minute with you."

"Why not?" Eli asked.

"Because she wants to kiss Daniel." Josh said in a singsong voice.

"Joshua!" Ellen scolded and slammed the door behind them.

Harper laughed. I was about to excuse myself and go upstairs when my phone buzzed with a text from Nick.

"Merry Christmas!"

I smiled and sent a text back. "Can't wait to see you!"

"Have you told them yet?"

"No, waiting for you." I replied.

Harper came over. "Mom, when do you need help starting dinner?"

"Not for a couple of hours. You go have fun."

She grabbed her coat and headed for the door. I loved having everyone here, but I was grateful for the quiet time as well, so I could clean up behind the kids and their discarded wrapping paper.

Harper came back to the kitchen. "Mom, come with me. We'll come back in time to start dinner, and I'll clean this up."

"Okay, but only if you promise to have me back in time to start dinner."

Tommy, Ellen, and the kids had already left in my car, so Harper drove us to the ice rink.

I was surprised to see so many people out and about on Christmas Day, and I noticed the clouds were gathering again. I also wondered if the lingering snow in the shadows was anticipating more snowfall.

"Grandma, come skate with us!"

"No, not today." I laughed.

Daniel was waiting for Harper when we arrived. She and Daniel joined Tommy, Ellen, and the boys. I was happy to watch. Then a low voice spoke in my ear.

"I thought that was you."

Nick, my heart did a somersault.

"I didn't think I would get to see you until later." I smiled, turning to him.

"I finished what I had to do early, and I was taking a stroll, when I spotted the most beautiful women in the world." He said with a dazzling smile. "Wanna skate?"

"Oh no, I don't want to fall and make a fool of myself."

"I promise you won't fall. Trust me?"

He stared deeply into my eyes. "Implicitly."

We walked over to the rental booth, laced up and hit the ice. Nick wrapped a protective arm around me and, true to his word, I did not fall. I'm not sure my skates were touching the ice either, but I was safe.

Tommy and Ellen stopped short and watched, and Nick and I made the circuit around the rink. Daniel and Harper took little notice, and the boys cheered. I couldn't tell what Tommy was thinking, but I could see he was surprised. I hadn't mentioned Nick to him yet. It just never seemed like the right time, and I didn't need his approval.

We went around once more, and Nick looked down at me. "Ready for a break?"

"Yes, please."

He guided me off the ice, and we sank down onto a bench.

"Whew! That was fun." I laughed.

"Yes, it was."

Nick returned the skates, and we sat and watched the others.

Tommy and Ellen skated over. I knew the sight of me sitting with a man drew their attention.

Tommy spoke up first, "Mom, everything alright?"

"Yes, very much so." Nick and I stood up. "Nick, this is my son Tommy, his wife Ellen."

Nick reached out to shake Tommy's hand. "This is my boyfriend. Nick Tanner." I smiled warmly at them.

Tommy's eyes narrowed.

Ellen smiled, "Boyfriend? Did I hear boyfriend?"

"Yes, that's right." I stared at Tommy, expecting a similar reaction from him as I got from Harper. But whatever he was going to say was overshadowed by Ellen's squeal.

"Oh, I am so happy for you! I can't believe you didn't tell me!"

"Nice to meet you." I heard Tommy say.

"You, too. Great looking kids." Nick nodded toward the boys.

"Thanks, they're a handful."

Nick chuckled, "They're supposed to be at that age."

Tommy turned back to check on the boys.

"What's wrong?" Ellen whispered, "You look worried."

"I guess I am expecting a negative reaction from Tommy. That is why I didn't mention it earlier."

"Don't you worry about him. He'll be fine." Ellen patted my arm before joining Tommy and the boys.

I stood watching. Nick looked down at me. "That went well."

Harper slid up next to me. "Mom, we need to get back to the house and start dinner."

"Okay, baby cakes." Harper drove us back to the house. Nick and Daniel followed in their cars, leaving Tommy, Ellen, and the boys to have a little more fun.

Nick was getting the fireplace going while Daniel started the coffee.

"Mom, tell me what you need me to do?" Harper stood in the middle of the kitchen looking around.

"I have prepped as much ahead as I could, but we need to get things in the oven." I pulled the turkey out and handed it to Harper. "Can you put this in the warmer so it doesn't dry out?"

"I didn't see you put this in the oven before we left." She smiled.

"You were busy. I knew we wouldn't have time to wait for it after we got back. Let's concentrate on the sides and desserts that need to go in."

"You got it."

I heard the boys when they came back from skating. Tommy did a good job of keeping the boys busy. I hoped he and Nick were getting along.

Ellen joined Harper and me in the kitchen to help.

I stole a glance towards the living room. "Should we be concerned about the lack of noise coming from the other room?"

Ellen gave me a smile. "I'll go check on everyone."

She was back a moment later. "They are all asleep."

"All of them?" I asked.

"Everyone. The football game appears to go just fine without them screaming at the T.V." She laughed.

"Well, that's a relief."

Harper came over and put an arm around me. "Don't worry. Tommy will like him. I do, too."

"Yes, but it took you a while."

"But I did come around and so will he. And you don't need our permission or approval."

"You're right." I smiled and slid an apple pie into the oven.

Finally, the various timers beeped, and the boys, large and small, woke up in time to help set the table.

Eli gave the blessing. Tommy and Nick seemed to have hit it off and the two of them, along with Daniel, talked football most of the time.

Christina joined us in time for dessert. And we all sat around enjoying coffee and pie.

"Mom, you made enough to feed an army." Harper looked at the leftovers on the kitchen counter and table.

"Which means I shouldn't have to cook for a week." I grinned. "There's a method to the madness."

After we cleaned the dishes, with the help of the boys, we returned to sit and enjoy the fire and the Christmas tree.

Ellen started corralling the boys for bedtime.

"I'll go with you." I said as she shooed them upstairs. My intention was to slip into my room to get the ring.

Ellen flopped down next to Tommy on the sofa. I hovered near the kitchen doorway.

"They've had a busy day." I smiled, enjoying having my family, or at least most of them here.

Nick stood up. "If I can have everyone's attention, please."

We all turned our attention to him. "Uh, Judy, if you could come stand next to me in front of the tree."

I looked around the room to see if anyone else had any idea what Nick was up to. Everyone looked curious.

I walked over to stand next to him as requested.

"I've told Judy this already, but I want you all to hear it. These past weeks have been the happiest of my life. I have never felt more whole, more complete, than I am with you. It has taken all our lives so far to find each other, but now that we have, I don't want to waste another minute. I've asked Judy to marry me."

To say they were in shock was an understatement. The four of them all blinked at him and then me for a moment. Ellen, Christina, and Harper jumped up and came over to hug.

Ellen asked, "Harper, did you know about this?"

"No, I had no idea." She turned to glare at Daniel. "Did you?"

He shrugged and grinned. "I knew he bought the ring. I didn't know when he was going to propose."

Harper frowned. "Well, it figures he knew. I had no idea he could be so sneaky."

"Your turn." I said to Harper.

Harper lowered her voice. "What? I don't know, Mom."

Ellen nodded towards Daniel. "I think you better consider it." She said as she squeezed Harper's hand.

CHAPTER 25

Harper

As the evening wound down and everyone gathered around the fire, I glanced at Daniel, who was nursing his glass of champagne on the couch. His laughter, warm and unrestrained, mingled with the others. I couldn't help but smile. It had been a long day, filled with love and chaos, but now I was wishing for a moment. I longed to have Daniel to myself.

I went over and sat next to him. "I think I've had enough for one night. What about you?"

"Absolutely," he replied without hesitation.

"Great! I'll let mom know we are leaving."

We said our goodbyes and bundled up against the frosty night air. The street was blanketed in a soft layer of snow, untouched since the earlier flurries. Christmas lights glowed warmly from the surrounding houses, their reflections shimmering on the icy ground.

Daniel walked me to my car.

"I'll follow you home to make sure you get there safely."

"Thank you."

We lingered for a moment, and I thought he was going to say more, but instead, he opened my car door. "Drive slowly on the roads. I'll follow you."

It took thirty minutes to get back to my apartment. The main roads were clear, but I was still nervous and was extra cautious. I breathed a sigh of relief when I pulled into the parking garage next to my apartment. Daniel parked next to me and came over to open my door.

Stepping out, I smiled awkwardly. "Thank you for following me. I get so nervous when the roads are like this."

"I didn't mind."

"Would you like to come up for a minute?"

He looked like he was struggling to decide.

"Or maybe a walk over to the park?" I offered him an out. But I had to admit I was disappointed that he hesitated.

He smiled down at me. "Are you up for it?"

"Yeah."

We strolled down the sidewalk to the park. Although the street tree lights were still on, the Christmas tree had been shut down for the night. The park was still pretty, even without the lights. I took a deep breath. The air was cold, but it felt good. It cleared away the heady cobwebs from all the heavy food and drink.

"I didn't realize how much I needed this," I admitted as we strolled around the central fountain. "It's been a perfect day, but... a little overwhelming, too."

Daniel chuckled; his hands tucked into his pockets. "I get that. Your family is amazing, though. Full of love—and a lot of energy."

I laughed, shaking my head. "That's one way to put it. But yeah, they are amazing. It just... reminds me of how much my life has shifted. Seeing Mom so happy, Tommy with Ellen and the boys... I wonder if I'm missing out on something."

Daniel stopped walking, turning to face me. His expression was soft but serious. "You're not missing out, Harper. You're finding your way. And for what it's worth... I'd like to be part of that."

My breath caught, visible in the chilly air between them. "Daniel..." I looked down, kicking the snow. "I'm not sure I'm good at this—relationships, I mean. I've always been so focused on being independent, and sometimes I think I push people away because of it."

Daniel reached out, gently lifting my chin so our eyes met. "I know. It's one thing I admire, actually—your strength. But you don't have to do everything alone, Harper. And you don't have to decide anything tonight. I just wanted you to know how I feel."

A light snow fell, dusting his dark hair with white. My heart thudded in my chest. "You always know the right thing to say, don't you?"

"Only when it matters," he replied, his voice soft.

My lips curved into a small smile as I stepped closer, slipping my hand into his. "Come on," she said. "Let's go back to my place. I think I have some leftover pie—and I don't feel like being alone tonight."

Daniel's grin widened. "Pie and company? You're spoiling me."

We walked back to my apartment. It felt cozy and warm after the intensity of mom's house with all the decorations and people. It had felt overwhelming by the end of the day. I turned on the Christmas tree, letting it provide a faint glow in the living room.

Looking around. "I wonder where Yeti was. Normally, he greets me at the door. Please make yourself comfortable while I check on him."

I walked down the hallway to my bedroom to find my little fluff ball asleep on my bed. I smiled and tiptoed up the hallway.

Daniel was relaxing on the couch. "Everything okay?"

"Yes, he's asleep. You stay there, I'll get us some pie."

"You sure you don't need some help?"

"I've totally got it."

I carried a tray of pie and milk back to the living room.

Joining him on the couch, I handed him a plate of pie and a fork. "It's nothing fancy."

For a while, we ate in comfortable silence. When Daniel set his empty plate on the coffee table, he turned to her, his expression unreadable. "Can I say something without you overthinking it?"

"Not promising anything," I teased, but my heart fluttered.

"I'm glad I could spend today with you. It's been the best Christmas I've had in a long time."

I looked down at my hands, the weight of his words settling over me. I took a deep breath, then looked up at him. "Me too."

The room seemed to grow quieter, the air between us charged. My heart pounded as Daniel leaned in slightly, giving me plenty of time to pull away. Instead, I closed the gap, my lips meeting his in a kiss that was soft but certain.

When he pulled back, I rested my forehead against his. "This scares me," I whispered. "But it also feels... right."

Daniel smiled, brushing a strand of hair behind my ear. "Then let's figure it out. Together."

We sat there for a while, watching the snow falling softly outside the window. For the first time in a long time, I felt something she hadn't dared to hope for: peace.

As the snow blanketed the world outside in a soft, fresh start, this Christmas wasn't just a holiday—it was the beginning of something new, something I never expected, but couldn't imagine it without Daniel.

The End

AUTHOR'S NOTE

Dear Reader,

Thank you for diving into *The Christmas Dilemma*! My love for small-town holiday traditions and the charm of Gates Point, a fictional town that holds a special place in my heart, inspired this story. Though Gates Point isn't real, I created it by combining what I consider some of the best parts of my hometown of Hampton, Virginia, and our neighboring city of Newport News. Virginia's maritime history and culture along the Chesapeake Bay, with its slower pace of life and brighter holiday magic, inspire the spirit of Gates Point.

While writing, I drew from experiences with rare snowfalls in the region surrounding Hampton and Newport News, the unique warmth of community holiday parades, and the universal challenges of balancing love and obligation during the busiest season of the year. If you've ever felt torn between the joy of giving and the weight of expectations, I hope this story resonated with you.

I'd also like to acknowledge the unsung heroes of small-town holiday events—the organizers, volunteers, the sponsors, and families who make these moments so memorable. Their dedication inspired the heart of this story.

Feel free to reach out and share your thoughts or your favorite holiday traditions at www.stichesandstories.com. I love hearing from readers and connecting through our shared love of stories.

May this book bring you joy, laughter, and a little holiday magic.

Warmly,

Lynn

ALSO BY LYNN STORY

Rescue My Love

The Primrose Heart

Ginny's Christmas Wish

Love at Bay

Her Private Chef

A Father for Christmas

A Gates Point Christmas Volume 1

The Maple Stree Cafe (Short Story)

Milton Keynes UK
Ingram Content Group UK Ltd.
UKHW022121091224
452185UK00010B/455

9 781736 787977